The Swing Era
The
Postwar
Years

TIME-LIFE BOOKS

FOUNDER: Henry R. Luce 1898-1967

Editor-in-Chief: Hedley Donovan
Chairman of the Board: Andrew Heiskell
President: James R. Shepley
Group Vice President: Rhett Austell

Vice Chairman: Roy E. Larsen

MANAGING EDITOR: Jerry Korn
Assistant Managing Editors: Ezra Bowen,
David Maness, Martin Mann, A. B. C. Whipple
Planning Director: Oliver E. Allen
Art Director: Sheldon Cotler
Chief of Research: Beatrice T. Dobie
Director of Photography: Melvin L. Scott
Senior Text Editor: Diana Hirsh
Assistant Art Director: Arnold C. Holeywell
Assistant Chief of Research: Myra Mangan

PUBLISHER: Joan D. Manley
General Manager: John D. McSweeney
Business Manager: John Steven Maxwell
Sales Director. Carl G. Jaeger
Promotion Director: Paul R. Stewart
Public Relations Director: Nicholas Benton

TIME-LIFE RECORDS

EDITOR: George G. Daniels
Editorial Staff for *The Swing Era: "Postwar Years":*
Editor: Philip W. Payne
Administrative Editor: Jeanne LeMonnier
Staff Writers: David Johnson, Joan S. Reiter, Michele Wood
Graphics: Leonard S. Levine
Researchers: Betty Ajemian, Lea Guyer, Suad A. McCoy,
Florence McNeil, Joan Nierenberg, Karl F. Reuling,
Barbara Richey, Eleanor Schwartz

EDITORIAL PRODUCTION

Production Editor: Douglas B. Graham
Assistant Production Editor: Gennaro C. Esposito
Quality Director: Robert L. Young
Assistant Quality Director: James J. Cox
Copy Staff: Rosalind Stubenberg (chief),
Rachel Tuckerman, Florence Keith
Picture Department: Dolores A. Littles
Traffic: Feliciano Madrid

THE SWING ERA is produced in the United States by TIME-LIFE RECORDS in cooperation with CAPITOL RECORDS, INC. David D. Cavanaugh, Executive Producer, Bill Miller, Associate Producer. Editions outside the United States and Canada are produced in cooperation with Electric & Musical Industries, Limited, London, England, or its affiliated companies.

ON THE COVER: Almost every Lindy Hop step had a name and a more or less prescribed form, but dancers made up their own steps, too. Kaye Popp and Stanley Catron demonstrate one such improvisation in this 1948 Gjon Mili shot taken for LIFE.

THE STORY OF GREAT MUSIC
CONCERTS OF GREAT MUSIC
TO THE MOON
BEETHOVEN BICENTENNIAL COLLECTION
THE SWING ERA
RICHARD WAGNER RING OF THE NIBELUNG
AS YOU REMEMBER THEM

The Swing Era

A Clutch of Characters

The Postwar Years

TIME-LIFE RECORDS
NEW YORK

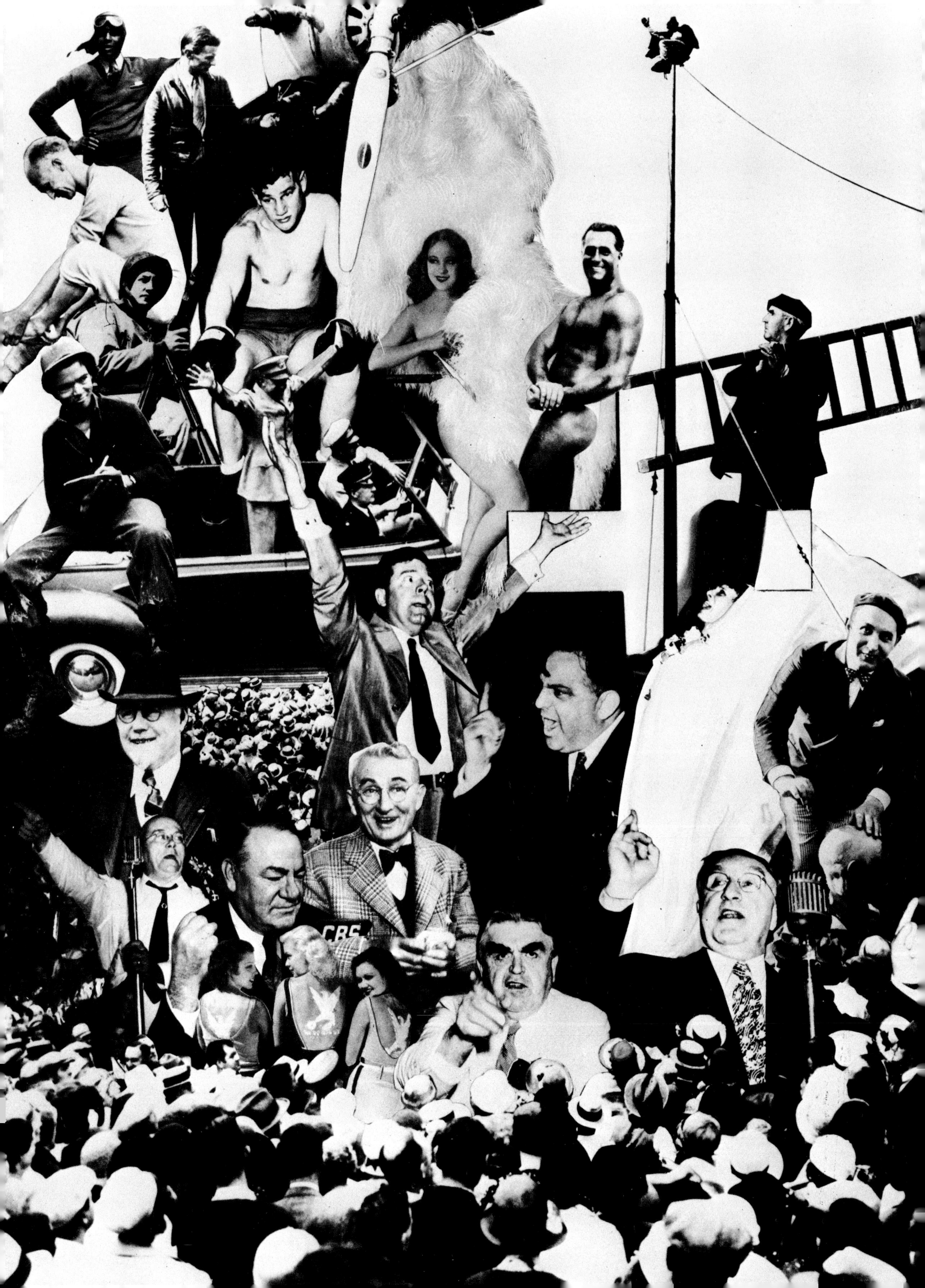
CBS

A Clutch
of Characters

Among the Swing Era people I remember best were the men and women whose life-styles gave tone and color to the period. The tone might be discordant, the color sometimes garish, but the dimensions of these figures were heroic. Some of them were indeed heroes, if humanly flawed. Some were real colorfast villains. Others were clowns or charlatans or gifted show-offs or simply superkooks. But they were all entertaining to have around.

Most of them are dead now and no one has really replaced them. They just don't make people like that anymore. It is as well that we have no more Senators like Theodore Bilbo, but it seems a shame not to have a few mayors like Fiorello La Guardia. Perhaps some of the great characters of the Swing Era were appropriate only to their own time. How many headlines could the wiliest gate-crasher or the most tenacious flagpole-sitter hope to inspire today? You have to fly to the moon or hijack an airplane now to get the kind of attention Douglas Corrigan got for making what he said was a simple navigational error or that Hubert Fauntleroy Julian got for playing a saxophone during a parachute jump.

Most of my personal favorites among the great characters of the Swing Era had a kind of comic-strip appeal and could have stepped into or out of "Our Boarding House" or "Mutt and Jeff" without significantly changing their outlines or their antics. People like Bilbo, La Guardia, Huey Long and "Ironpants" Johnson even looked as though they had been designed by cartoonists, just as the baseball players in those days seemed to have been invented by Ring Lardner. Perhaps we have grown up so much since then that comic-strip characters are now out of place in real life. I think we were more willing then to take a joke. We were also more innocently and earnestly seeking after heroes and heroines, and we found them. Individuals, not groups, stood out then and many of them stood out so far they eventually toppled over. But whether they made us laugh or cry or grind our teeth, they were part of the texture of life in the Swing Era.

Aimee Semple McPherson was the most glamorous evangelist the nation has ever known. Her Foursquare Gospel featured love, light and ecstasy with just a dash of faith healing. Aimee transcended her rather vague and elementary precepts as she swept onstage to the strains of rousing revivalist music in theaters and municipal auditoriums across the land, clad in clinging white with her arms full of red roses and a Bible tucked in one armpit. Her minions seemed to pass the plate about every twenty minutes while "Sister Aimee," as she liked to be called, asked for a "silent collection." A nickel dropped into one of the tin pie plates she provided would have rattled the rafters, so anybody in the crowd who had a dollar bill felt honor bound to surrender it to God — or to Aimee Semple McPherson.

She had auburn hair, a prominent nose, a mesmerizing voice and a burning desire to save souls. She seemed to have appeared, full-blown, out of Nowhere, Canada, at the end of World War I with ten dollars and a tambourine. Actually, Aimee Elizabeth Kennedy was born on a farm near Ingersoll, Ontario, on October 9, 1890, only child of a Methodist farmer and a former Salvation Army lassie. At seventeen she married Robert Semple, a husky boilermaker and a Holy Roller missionary who took her to China where he died of malaria a month before their daughter, Roberta Star, was born. Back in the United States, she married a grocery clerk named Harold McPherson and bore him a son, Rolf.

In 1918 she hit the road as a revivalist with her mother, two children and a tent, and wound up in Los Angeles where within two weeks she had rented and filled a 3,500-seat auditorium. After that, though her revivals carried her as far afield as Australia and New Zealand, she visited California every year and in 1921 struck gold, so to speak, in San Diego. During her sermon there a crippled woman rose from her wheelchair claiming to have been healed. Aimee's fame as a faith healer spread. She gave up her tent and with $1,500,000 donated by the faithful built the 5,000-seat Angelus Temple, topped with a lighted cross visible for fifty miles around. The temple drew worshipers like moths. McPherson had divorced her, saying he could not abide her "wildcat habits" at home, but hardly anybody noticed.

The gospel kept on spreading, fanned by near-hysterical shouting and singing sessions, "speaking in voices," elaborate dramatics and sensational entrances by Aimee dressed as a traffic cop, an admiral or a football player, or borne on the shoulders of admirers in a wicker chair laced with roses and looking somewhat like the Pope in Rome in his *sedia gestatoria*. Aimee

had folks "accepting Christ" in droves. Crutches and other discarded aids to the afflicted piled up in the Temple's Miracle Room. Her $25,000 radio station, KFSG, broadcast her message for 1,000 miles. She toured Europe and the Holy Land until British authorities threw her out of Palestine.

When Aimee disappeared from a seaside tent near Venice Beach, California, in 1926, hysterical followers held an all-night prayer meeting on the beach, strung searchlights and hurled themselves into the surf to search for her. Two men died in the search and a young girl killed herself. Aimee turned up miraculously on the Arizona border thirty-six days later with a story of having hiked for thirteen hours across the desert after

Clutching her Bible and flinging wide her arms, Aimee preaches to 20,000 people at the outdoor Organ Thea-

ter in Balboa Park on July 18, 1935. That was Aimee Semple McPherson Day at the San Diego World's Fair.

Aimee soothes an ecstatic delegate to 1942 Holy Ghost Rally in her Angelus Temple. For hours the faithful danced, spoke in tongues, fell prostrate. "If there's a fire under you," said Aimee, "you just can't sit still."

escaping from kidnappers in Mexico. But her shoes were oddly unscuffed, her coils of hair were neat and shining and such evidences of travail as she displayed were superficial. Fifty thousand people met the train when Aimee returned to Los Angeles and another 100,000 watched her motorcade tool off to the Temple. Less enraptured was District Attorney Asa Keyes, who uncovered considerable evidence that Aimee had spent a lot of those thirty-six days with Kenneth Ormiston, the Temple's radio operator. Keyes charged Aimee and her mother with obstructing justice. "I am being crucified by the very bats of hell," said Aimee. Her followers rejoiced when Keyes dropped the case just as he seemed to have it sewed up; they undoubtedly credited divine retribution when he later went to jail for taking a bribe. Aimee harbored no public resentment. "I only remember the hours when the sun shines, sister," said she.

The sun shone again when she eloped — by air, of course, for she wasn't one to climb prosaically out of a second-story window on a ladder — with a roly-poly baritone named David I. Hutton, whose only previous claim to attention had been his rendition of the part of the Pharaoh in one of the six operas Aimee wrote for Angelus Temple production. This marriage ended in divorce, suit and countersuit. Throughout the '30s, Aimee was in court as often as she was in church: she had tax troubles over proceeds of the Temple; she and Hutton sued a Panamanian bartender for having named a "Hallelujah cocktail" in her honor; she was embroiled in a breach-of-promise suit brought against Hutton and in slander suits brought against her lawyer by her own daughter, by the publicity agent for the Temple and by a Mrs. Rheba Crawford Splivalo, "the angel of Broadway," a onetime fellow preacher at the Temple. She even had a seven-year slanging match with her mother, the formidable Mrs. Minnie ("Ma") Kennedy who accused Aimee of punching her in the nose. Aimee accused Ma of having tossed a boa constrictor into her room.

Even their gold bridgework

Throughout all these vicissitudes the faithful rallied time and again to Aimee's calls for "defense funds." Into her collection plates they tossed their money, their jewelry, even their bridgework if it contained some usable gold. In 1944, at almost fifty-four, she made her last appearance before a warmly receptive crowd in Oakland, California. She died soon after, apparently the victim of an accidental overdose of sleeping pills. Noted the Los Angeles Daily News, duly grateful for the reams of copy she had provided over the years, "Aimee Semple McPherson yesterday went to meet the Lord whose greatest press agent she had been for nearly thirty-five years."

If you missed getting your soul laundered by Aimee McPherson you had a chance to become at least a self-trained social lion under the guidance of Dale Carnegie, a Missouri boy who spent his first twenty years on a corn-and-hog farm, practicing elocution as he rode to school every day on horseback. Carnegie had failed as a truck salesman and as an actor when he emerged in New York City in 1912, teaching night classes in speech at the 125th Street Y.M.C.A., admission two dollars. He was an instant success. His lectures evolved into the Dale Carnegie Institute of Effective Speech and Human Relations. In the mid-'30s he published his collected lectures as a book — How To Win Friends and Influence People. Reviewers either ignored it or sniffed at it, and syndicated columnist Heywood Broun said he found Carnegie eminently resistible. But would-be friends and influencers bought the book so fast that for a time it was second only to the Bible as America's nonfiction best seller. The U.S.

Bureau of Prisons ordered two hundred copies for distribution to the libraries of all its prisons including the maximum-security jails at Leavenworth, Atlanta and Alcatraz. It was eventually translated into more than thirty languages and sold twelve million copies.

Carnegie settled down in well-heeled comfort in Forest Hills, New York, with a second wife who promptly turned out a best seller of her own called *How To Help Your Husband Get Ahead.* He remained much in demand as a public speaker in such places as Constitution Hall and Carnegie Hall (no kin), wrote an inspirational column six days a week for the newspapers, talked on radio, and at sixty-three sired a daughter.

Carnegie's works inspired thousands of ecstatic testimonials: "In the past four years I had three jobs and was fired from all of them. I bought a grocery store. . . . Now, having taken half the [Carnegie] course, I have already increased my sales from $500 to $700 a week."

"I was a hot-air balloon. Before taking the course every speech I made was a flop. After taking the course every speech I made was a success."

But Carnegie himself probably supplied his own best epitaph in *How To Win Friends:* "How I wish such a book as this had been placed in my hands twenty years ago! What a priceless boon it would have been!"

Even more popular than Carnegie, over the long haul, was the work of Robert L. Ripley, who for thirty-one years made his living by presenting in words and drawings an endless stream of unlikely facts and occurrences. LeRoy Ripley was a poor boy from California who used to pitch and make posters for a semipro baseball team. His poster art got him a job as a sports cartoonist. He landed eventually on the New York *Globe* where his employers renamed him "Robert" which seemed to them a manlier handle than "LeRoy."

One day, when hard-pressed for a subject for his cartoon panel, Ripley scratched together some offbeat sports performances and labeled the effort "Champs and Chumps," a title he changed at the last minute to "Believe It Or Not." People liked it so much that the feature became his career. It appeared, at the height of its syndicated popularity, in eight languages and 328 newspapers in the U.S. and abroad, and supplied the substance of seventeen books, 1,200 radio broadcasts, 105 five-minute TV shows, six Barnum-like museums and countless lectures and other public appearances.

If a reader doubted that J. Ogden Armour lost a million dollars a day for 130 days, he could send Ripley a stamped, self-addressed envelope and back would come proof. At least, this was how it was supposed to work after King Features got Ripley organized and assembled a staff to handle the one million letters sent to Ripley every year. Before that, Ripley had begun by simply throwing away all mail except letters from

DRAWING BY GEO. PRICE; COPR. © 1938, 1966 THE NEW YORKER MAGAZINE, INC.

"They're friends — leftovers from the old Dale Carnegie days," says a 1938 cartoon (*above*). Actually, Carnegie was still going strong and continuing to make friends. Below, Carnegie and an unidentified lady tourist chat with a bearded saddhu, or holy man, during a 1939 visit to a Hindu colony in Port-of-Spain, Trinidad.

his immediate family. Later he took to answering some mail, years late, storing thousands of unread letters in his attic and, as he restlessly roved the world, throwing still other letters out of airplanes. (Some airplanes then had open cockpits or openable windows.) His undaunted correspondents kept writing. Once Mr. Ripley immortalized a Michigan woman who had discovered a radish growing out of a carrot. After reading this item, an Iowa produce dealer, named Wayne Harbour, thereafter diligently wrote to just about every living soul mentioned in "Believe It Or Not" to inquire about the accuracy of Ripley's claims. Mr. Harbour reported that Mr. Ripley was right 99% of the time.

Lindbergh, the 67th pond-hopper

Ripley loved to catch his readers on technicalities. Three days after Charles Lindbergh's historic flight, Ripley asserted that "Lindbergh was the 67th man to make a nonstop flight over the Atlantic Ocean." Thousands of indignant readers phoned and wrote in, only to learn that Lindbergh had been preceded across the pond by one airplane containing two men and two dirigibles containing a total of sixty-four men.

He also provided an additional push to a campaign long waged by others to add status to a patriotic song. Ripley announced in 1929 that *The Star-Spangled Banner* was not, officially, the U.S. national anthem. Five million disturbed readers petitioned Congress to make it official and this was done in 1931. When he revealed that Lord Byron's dog had a tombstone though the poet had none, English schoolchildren raised money to mark Byron's grave.

Not all Ripley's correspondents were skeptics. Every farmer whose herd produced a two-headed calf, every woman who found a long-lost engagement ring embedded in the world's biggest carrot, felt impelled to write to Ripley about it immediately. Some folks waggishly addressed their letters "To the Biggest Liar in the World" or in lieu of an address drew pictures on the envelope of a bee, a leaf, an oar and a knot. Whenever Ripley noted in his panel that some such letter had been "promptly delivered" it naturally inspired further efforts. In 1930 Postmaster General Walter F. Brown put his foot down, saying that postal clerks were spending too much time decoding this foolishness and that such mail would thereafter go to the dead-letter office.

Ripley got from his correspondents and from a staff of researchers most of the ideas for the oddities he chronicled. (He insisted on calling them "oddities," never "freaks"; he defined an oddity as "a high class freak.") Sometimes he himself traveled to remote spots to check out particularly obscure facts, and he had a great fancy for making broadcasts from places like a snake pit or the North Pole.

Before he died in 1949, Ripley presented a magnificent collection of Oriental art to Dartmouth College,

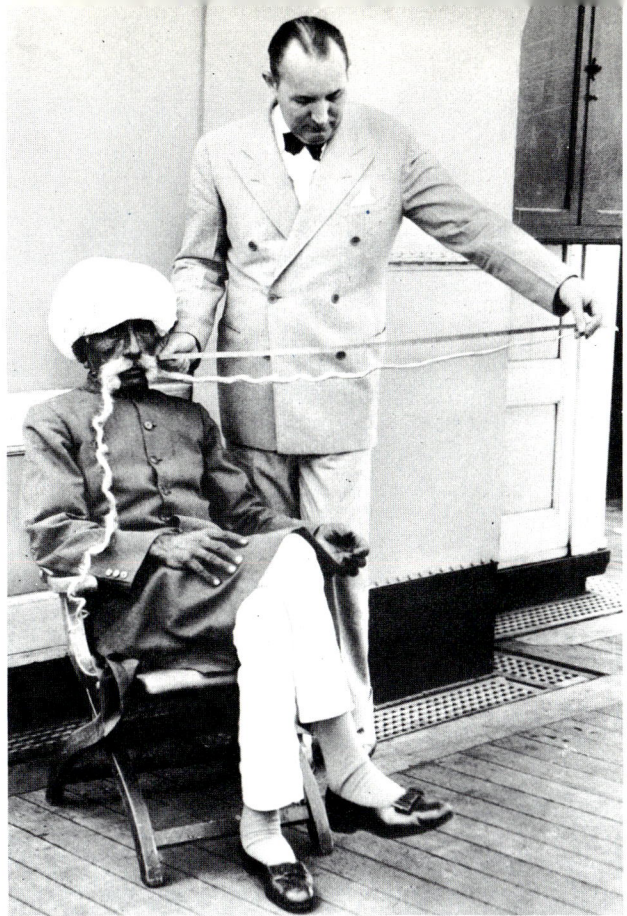

Above, Robert L. Ripley measures what he claimed was the world's longest mustache. All 103 inches of it belonged to policeman Desar Arjan Dangar of Kathiawar, India. In one of his most famous cartoons (*below*), Ripley figured that the birth rate of an estimated 600 million Chinese could keep them marching forever.

Ripley's— Believe It or Not!

THE MARCHING CHINESE

IF ALL THE **CHINESE** IN THE WORLD WERE TO MARCH -4 ABREAST- PAST A GIVEN POINT THEY WOULD **NEVER** FINISH PASSING THOUGH THEY MARCHED FOREVER AND EVER! (Based on U.S. Army Marching Regulations)

Angelo Siciliano at fifteen (*left*) was a spindly ninety-seven-pound weakling who once had sand kicked in his face by a bully at the beach. But he learned to build muscles and became Charles Atlas. Through ads (*center*) which hardly changed for 50 years, he invited the world to share his discovery, and many people did. Atlas himself, as a 1964 picture (*right*) shows, remained a stunning hunk of beefcake at past seventy.

one of several institutions that had given him honorary degrees, possibly in recognition of his scholarly researches into Mother Goose. Wee Willie Winkie, he reported, was really William III of Orange and Humpty Dumpty was Richard III.

Aimee saved souls; Carnegie and Ripley worked on minds; Charles Atlas dealt with bodies. Nobody within reach of a Sunday supplement or a pulp magazine could miss his bulging muscles. He beamed out, suntanned, cheerful, invincible, sometimes balancing the world on his back, and he offered help for every "ninety-seven-pound weakling" in the world. His classic advertisement showed a beach, where a well-built youth kicked sand all over a weakling and made off with his girl. It was enough to terrify any nervous adolescent into glancing surreptitiously into the mirror. And *that* was enough to make him sit right down, clip the coupon, and "send off," as we used to say, for Atlas' free illustrated booklet on body-building.

To prove he wasn't a figment of a photo retoucher's imagination, Atlas once pulled six automobiles, chained together, for a full mile. Another time he hauled a 72½-ton railway car for 112 feet down a track on the end of a rope. He was real, all right, but his name wasn't: he was born Angelo Siciliano in Acri, Italy, and as an immigrant boy in Brooklyn he weighed exactly ninety-seven pounds at age fifteen and was in constant peril of being beaten up by bigger boys.

A visit to the Brooklyn Museum inspired him to develop muscles like those he saw on some of the statues. He began working out at a local gym, but his real start in life, he always said, came from watching a lion in the Bronx Zoo. He wondered how such a big beast could keep his muscles in shape in such a confined space. Then the lion stood up and stretched, and sharp-eyed Angelo saw how the animal braced one muscle against another in a thorough kind of stretching and toning exercise. The boy rushed home and tried out the lion's system. Magically, his muscles began to grow. Before long he was all but bursting out of his suit jackets.

Atlas became first a combination strong man and

janitor in a Coney Island sideshow and then a full-time model, retained by a number of sculptors. A couple of sculptors persuaded Atlas to enter Bernarr MacFadden's competition for The World's Most Perfectly Developed Man. Atlas bought a secondhand leopardskin loincloth and sent the millionaire publisher of *Physical Culture* magazine a few pictures of himself. He won the contest and, further encouraged by his sculptor friends, legally changed his name to Charles Atlas and started selling muscles by mail. With the help of Charles Roman, a young advertising man, he developed his "dynamic tension" system into an elaborate set of dietary and conditioning instructions, including such options as a ten-volume *Encyclopedia of Hygienics*. The Atlas system gradually eliminated all his major competitors, including one who went to Washington and stood on his thumbs for the Federal Trade Commission to prove the superiority of his ideas. Men and women all over the world signed up with Atlas. His students included boxer Max Baer and comedian Fred Allen. Atlas even sent some helpful hints to Mahatma Gandhi, apparently without effect since Gandhi remained a ninety-seven pound weakling.

When he died at 80, Atlas was the head of a flourishing business conducted in seven languages which got some 35,000 registrants a year from the U.S. alone. Late in life, he still got appreciative "ahs" when he worked out on the beach of Florida where he spent his winters —and nobody ever kicked sand in his face.

The Atlas system really works; the contributions to science of Dr. John R. ("Goat Gland") Brinkley are more doubtful. Gentlemanly Arthur Krock of the New York *Times* said Brinkley was "famous for his method of renewing the youth of senescent Kansans by borrowing vitality from the caprine species." What the doctor did was transplant bits of goat gland into human testicles. He apparently got the idea as a young doctor in Milford, Kansas, when a goat-farming patient complained of acute lassitude and audibly envied the rather spectacular sexual energy of his goats. Eureka! thought Brinkley. Before long he had more patients than he could handle at $750 to $1,500 per operation.

He built a big hospital in Milford and an elaborate house and purchased a fleet of Cadillacs and a yacht or two. He bought a radio station to advertise his specialty. Milford boomed; the post office had to be expanded to handle the 3,000 letters a day that poured in for Dr. Brinkley. The doc let his clients choose their own goats from among his flock, in a sort of bizarre surgical application of the theatrical audition. "Operations performed according to your own selection," he said. "You pay only for what you choose."

Once the goat business and the radio got going well, Brinkley branched out into diagnosis and prescription by radio. He provided some 1,500 druggists in Kansas and neighboring states with coded lists of prescriptions, and dispensed the basic ingredients through his own Milford Drug Company. On his regular radio program he urged listeners to write or phone him their symptoms; he prescribed treatment by air.

"This little lady has been seeing spots before her eyes, has occasional dizzy spells and is constipated," went a typical broadcast. "Prescriptions 66 and 74, which she can procure at the Acme drugstore at $5 and $7 each, will bring her relief."

Before long the American Medical Association and its fighting Dr. Morris Fishbein were hot on his trail. The concerted medical and legal attacks against him went on for years. The only medical degree Brinkley could produce was one from a short-lived diploma mill in Kansas City, Missouri, called the Eclectic Medical University. He had, it developed, begun life in North Carolina, become a telegraph operator, collected a degree from Eclectic and hung out his sign in Milford.

Brinkley defended himself passionately, producing for medical examining boards a parade of satisfied clients. One stalwart actually swore that, although he had been impotent for years, Dr. Brinkley's operation had so restored his powers that his wife had given birth to a bouncing baby boy. This son was named, incredibly, Billy.

From the middle '20s until he died in 1942, Goat Gland Brinkley was under constant attack, but he gave ground slowly. First he lost his Kansas license to practice, then he lost his radio station KFKB (for "Kansas First, Kansas Best") and retreated to Del Rio, Texas. From there he directed a Mexican radio station, XER, which was out of the reach of U.S. authorities and so powerful that it drowned out every other station for miles. He continued his radio prescriptions via XER and branched out into the "treatment" of cancer, of disease of the urinary tract, or any other ailment anybody could think up. He was still doing so well in 1939 that when he sued Dr. Fishbein of the AMA for libel that year, his chief argument was that a Fishbein article calling him a "quack" had reduced his income from $1,100,000 in 1937 to $210,000 in 1938.

'Irresistible to the moron mind'

While he lasted, no man of the era gave free enterprise — or goats — such a run for its money and, if only his devoted followers had known how to spell, the incredible Dr. Brinkley might have ended up running for President as well. "He is irresistible to the moron mind," said editor William Allen White. Twice he was nearly elected governor of Kansas, once running against Alfred M. Landon, the "Kansas Sunflower" who eventually lost a 1936 race for President to Franklin Delano Roosevelt.

The first time he entered the race, he was too late to be listed on the ballot and he implored his radio listeners to write in his name. Thousands of them did, but it turned out they could hear better than they could write: Goat-Gland Brinkley, who had campaigned for free textbooks, a lake in every county, and "let's pasture goats on the statehouse lawn," always claimed that 50,000 ballots for him were thrown out because voters had misspelled his name.

In the late '30s the roof fell in on Brinkley. A hospital he started in Little Rock, Arkansas, never quite got off the ground; the federal government closed in with a $200,000 tax claim; the Mexican radio station's expenses mounted drastically and, after Brinkley fired an employee whose father had considerable political influence, malpractice suits against Brinkley proliferated. The authorities cracked down on him for allegedly looting the assets of an "aircraft school" he had bought and the U.S. Post Office sued him for fraud. He transferred most of his considerable worldly possessions to his family and some trusted employees and died technically bankrupt, thoroughly discredited and memorialized by his old enemy, Dr. Fishbein, as "the greatest charlatan in medical history."

Theodore Gilmore ("The Man") Bilbo did better with the voters than Dr. Brinkley, though his redeeming qualities, whatever they were, seemed to escape everyone but his constituents. Bilbo was a stocky little pecan-grower who liked to compare himself to Napo-

leon. At thirty he was elected state senator and soon created his first political scandal by admitting to bribe-taking. The state senate denounced him as "unfit to sit with honest, upright men in this respectable legislative body," and asked him to resign. Instead, he built a formidable political machine and became Governor and then U.S. Senator.

As Mississippi's $7,500-a-year Governor he built a $75,000 mansion he called his "Dream House." He also fired 179 state college professors at one swoop. Outraged students burned him in effigy. On another occasion, he refused to convene the legislature for fear it would impeach him.

He was an avowed member of the Ku Klux Klan and a shameless racist who once proposed — apparently in all seriousness — taking 400,000 square miles of African colonies away from France and Great Britain and resettling there eight million of the then twelve million U.S. Negroes. In a numbing three-and-a-half-hour speech on the floor of the U.S. Senate in 1939, he claimed that the blacks were overwhelmingly in favor of the plan. The "Bilbonic plague," as he was sometimes called, spewed out a stream of public invective against blacks, Jews and Italians (whom he occasionally addressed as "My dear Dago").

Sample Bilbo letter of the time: "Dear Mr. Golditch,

To credulous thousands, John R. Brinkley (*left*) looked and sounded like a doctor. He took in $12,000,000 by implanting goat gonads in men to increase their virility. Patients selected donors from among Brinkley's flock of nearly odorless Toggenberg goats (*below*); Angoras, he had found, gave recipients a permanent smell.

I notice that you are the secretary of the National Committee to Combat Anti-Semitism. Now, let me tell you that if you would quit lining up with these Communists and negroes in New York City, who are trying to put through the American Congress such fool, crack-brain, legislative monstrosities as FEPC [the Fair Employment Practices Act] and so forth, you would not need a committee to combat anti-semitism . . . there are just a few of you New York Jew "kikes" that are fraternizing and socializing with the negroes for selfish and political reasons . . . you had better stop and think."

A red tie and a well-advertised sex life

At election time he roared through Mississippi, in an old car, sporting a bright red necktie and a diamond-studded horseshoe stickpin and chatted in a folksy way with the voters, enough of whom loved it to keep him in office. His face carried the scars of a pistol-whipping suffered early in life and he was generally unprepossessing but politically effective. When opponents spread stories about his sex life (his wife had divorced him), Senator Bilbo publicly advertised for a suitable consort. He told an all-female audience that "If these stories about The Man Bilbo are true, you've got to admit, Sisters, he's a MAN."

He narrowly escaped being tossed out of the Senate for misconduct in 1947. Then, in one of those gentlemen's-club deals for which the Senate was famous, he was allowed instead to retire to Mississippi uncensured. He died soon after of various complications while recuperating from an operation for cancer of the mouth.

Huey Pierce Long lacked Bilbo's venom and took a generally more ample approach to life. He promised to make every man a king. He himself was "The Kingfish," so nicknamed by cronies for a character on the *Amos 'n' Andy* radio show who had a genius for avoiding honest labor.

It was in 1930 that Governor Long of Louisiana opted to give the rest of the nation the benefit of *his* genius. He was elected to the Senate, partly as a result of the convenient kidnapping, just before election time, of a couple of fellows who knew a little too much about Long. He then proceeded to mesmerize, scandalize and terrorize the U.S. populace as no demagogue was to do again until the time of Senator Joseph McCarthy.

Huey Long was part boor, part comedian, all action: he once received the press clad in lavender silk pajamas, and he once cockily wore a rakish straw hat throughout a meeting with President Roosevelt. He bragged about his record as Governor — 600,000 free schoolbooks distributed, 2,300 miles of road paved, 111 bridges built. He shrugged off the fact that he had in the process multiplied the Louisiana state debt by ten along with suspicions that he had increased his own wealth by some considerable factor. "There may be smarter people than me," he liked to say, "but they ain't in Louisiana."

He had a plan for ending the Depression: a fixed allowance of not less than one third of a mythical national average family wealth for every family. Though it didn't find much legislative favor, this was the heart of the slogan he blatted for years, "Share our wealth," and he proposed to do it by a federal confiscation and "reduction of swollen fortunes from the top."

He could roll out sonorous, if fractured, phrases, as in a 1935 letter to Roosevelt urging share-the-wealth legislation: "I am more than willing — yes, more desiring that whatever person in power who wishes to save the lives of 125,000,000 people affected by the maldistribution of wealth, in order that he may save his own political stakes, shall have all glory and all profit therefrom, undiminished."

He could get all cute and down-homey in comparing Presidents Hoover and Roosevelt. "Hoover is a hoot owl and Roosevelt is a scrootch owl. A hoot owl bangs into the nest and knocks the hen clean off and catches her while she's falling. But a scrootch owl slips into the roost and scrootches up to the hen and talks softly to her. And the hen just falls in love with him, and the next thing you know, there ain't no hen."

Long aimed for the presidency and quite a few people thought he might make it. The idea so dismayed Sinclair Lewis that he wrote a novel about a Fascist takeover of America. The central character sounded exactly like Huey Long, just as the protagonist did in a much better novel written later by Robert Penn Warren. But

"There is no worse influence in high life," said the New Orleans *Item* of Theodore Bilbo, here campaigning in Collins, Mississippi, in 1946 for a third Senate term. In spite of his critics, racist Bilbo won again.

Weary Huey Long (*above*) grins exultantly, though his fifteen-and-a-half-hour filibuster has failed to kill a 1935 bill supporting NRA. Many admired the Louisiana Senator's orations; after his assassination that same year, some 100,000 people came to his funeral (*right*) at the skyscraper capitol he built in Baton Rouge.

on September 8, 1935, the "smartest man in Louisiana" was fatally shot in the corridor of his own state capitol in Baton Rouge by a young dentist whose motives have never been satisfactorily explained.

Huey never made it to the White House, but his influence lingered. His brother Earl remained a power in Louisiana politics until his death in 1960. Many a protégé of the Kingfish represented Louisiana in the halls of Congress and his son Russell still sits in the Senate.

While Long was spouting in the Senate, Fiorello La Guardia was busy shaking New York City to its bedrock foundations. La Guardia grew up riding cayuses in Arizona and planned to become a jockey. No, said his Army bandmaster father, a musician. They compro-mised, and Fiorello entered the consular service. He worked in Budapest and Fiume and mastered French, German, Italian and some Balkan dialects. He returned to his native New York, became a lawyer, learned to fly airplanes only slightly more advanced than box kites and found his real field — politics. In 1916 he went to Washington for the first of seven terms as a Representative.

The next year he was off to Italy as a first lieutenant in the Aviation Section of the U.S. Signal Corps. He was the sloppiest-looking soldier you ever saw, but he trained American pilots, flew combat missions and in general behaved like the commander-in-chief of American forces in Italy. The West Point major who was

In 1932 President Herbert Hoover ordered General Douglas MacArthur and the U.S. Army to clear the "Bonus Marchers" out of Washington. The Marchers were World War I veterans, hard hit by the Depression, who wanted an advance payment on a promised bonus. Hoover opposed any such payment. He could find money to prop up failing banks and to provide farmers with seed and cattle feed, but he felt that giving money directly to people would be a degrading, soul-destroying "dole." La Guardia hit the roof. "I can go down to the market here and buy a parrot for two dollars. And in one day I can teach it to say 'Dole, Dole, Dole,'" he shrieked in his rather high voice, "but that parrot would never understand an economic problem."

Several million people agreed with La Guardia and some of them lived in New York. Fiorello had lost a 1929 race for mayor against the wisecracking incumbent, James J. Walker, but he ran again in 1933 and won. Walker had resigned under a cloud, La Guardia's two opponents split the vote, and Fiorello became New York's 101st mayor.

'Just treat me like Toscanini'

He set a stiff pace from the outset. On election night he heard that his Tammany Hall opponents were forcibly preventing his supporters from voting. He stormed into a polling place and offered to take on about twenty thugs with his bare hands. Police rescued him, and for their "interference" he threatened to kick them off the force when he got into office. He never did, but the minute he was sworn in he ordered the arrest of the city's most notorious criminal, Lucky Luciano.

For twelve years he bounced around New York, his paunch bobbing, his glasses thrust up on top of his head, his pugnacious jaw either thrust forward at malefactors or tucked downward with a puckish smile toward all citizens who were good and true. He seemed to turn up at every fire, parade and construction project in town, wearing as many different hats as Hedda Hopper. He conducted municipal bands, and when asked once if he wanted a spotlight on him replied, "Hell no! Just treat me like Toscanini."

He notably reduced crime and corruption — and the numbers of pushcart peddlers and organ grinders on the streets; he thought they tarnished the Italian-American image. "Around him there is always chaos, dust and smoke," said *The New Yorker*, but out of the chaos he produced more public projects than any administration ever had and left New York with a flock of new schools, bridges, parks, piers and low-cost public housing. He died two years after retiring from office in 1945.

John Llewellyn Lewis looked like a heavier-duty model from the same bulldozer assembly line that produced Fiorello La Guardia. He sounded like a cross between the prophet Isaiah and a bull fiddle. After finishing the seventh grade in his native Iowa, he be-

theoretically his superior fumed unavailingly about him in dispatches. La Guardia wound up a major himself and got the Italian War Cross from King Victor Emmanuel whom he thereafter called "Manny."

Back in the House of Representatives, he caused constant commotion by defending the public weal — or, in some cases, veal. During a speech about the high cost of living, he pulled a chop and a steak from his pockets and waved them at his fellow legislators to show how little consumers were getting for their money. Though technically a Republican, he favored minimum-wage and child-labor laws, the five-day week, unemployment insurance, publicly owned power and regulation of security exchanges.

New York's Mayor Fiorello La Guardia occasionally enjoyed a quiet moment and a good cigar at his City Hall desk (*below*), but more often he was out among the people in a variety of hats, expressions and antics, as in the study in perpetual motion at right. With equal aplomb, the mayor could conduct the Sanitation Department band (1), inspire his firemen amid a holocaust (2), inspect the digging of the Lincoln Tunnel (3), or climb a ladder to wield the first blowtorch in the demolition of the Second Avenue "El" (4). He was always acting, whether appearing in a skit he himself wrote to explain the operation of the federal food stamp plan (5) or making like a G-man while inspecting a cache of illicit arms (6) or tossing out the first ball of the season (7) or pleading his city's cause before the New York State Legislature (8).

Fiorello attacked with gusto a hot dog at the 1939 World's Fair (9), a dirty street during a cleanup campaign for the Fair's reopening in 1940 (10), and some breach of security as an air raid warden during a 1942 alert (11). He was calmer as a subway motorman (12) or as a bus driver (13), but he swung a mean sledge against illegal slot machines (14), peeled potatoes with deep concentration in a 1941 cooking class (15) and, with iron determination, conferred with Fire Department officials (16) during Harlem's 1943 race riots.

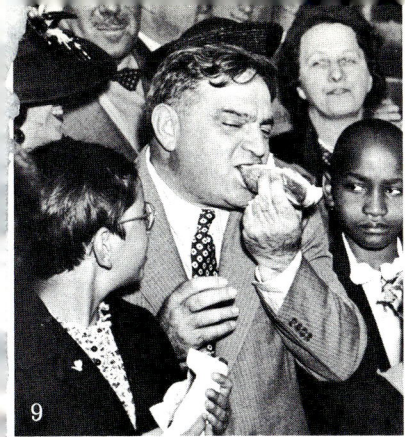

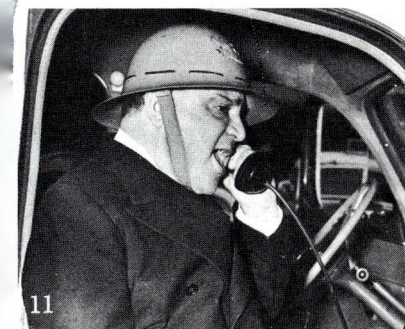

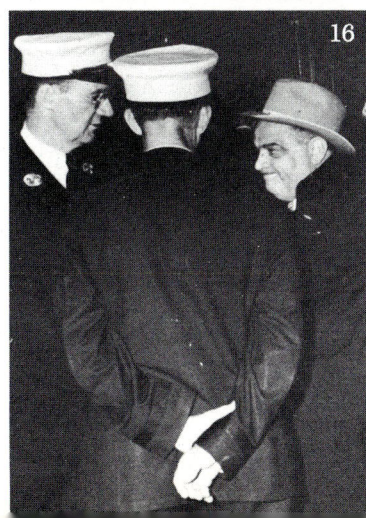

came a miner, a trade from which his father had been blacklisted for being a union organizer. After thirteen years underground, John L. surfaced as a lobbyist for the United Mine Workers in Springfield, Illinois, and soon rose to the top levels of both the U.M.W. and the American Federation of Labor. He read widely, retained much and frequently quoted Shakespeare, Karl Marx, the Bible, the *Iliad* and Oswald Spengler.

"Labor, like Israel," he would intone, "has many sorrows. Its women weep for their fallen, and they lament for the future of the race." Lewis was more prone to attack than to lament. He resembled a bulldog at bay and he had eyebrows like the fenders they put on cars in those days — enormous, flaring, aggressive. He threw his tanklike support behind the New Deal's efforts to enhance the rights of labor in the National Industrial Recovery Act of 1933 and the NRA industrial codes. When he suspected Vice President John Nance Garner of thwarting labor's aims, he thundered: "The genesis of this campaign against labor . . . emanates from a labor-baiting, poker-playing, whiskey-drinking, evil old man whose name is Garner." Garner's "knife," he said, "is searching for the quivering, pulsating heart of labor." At that, "Cactus Jack" Garner got off easy compared with William Green, the conservative head of the A. F. of L., who opposed Lewis' drive to reorganize labor by converting a multitude of small craft unions into a few huge industrial unions. "I have done a lot of exploring of Bill's mind," said Lewis, "and I give you my word there is nothing there." On another occasion, he intimated that Green's A. F. of L. had no head — just a neck that had "haired over."

A new flowering of the sit-down

With a handful of other labor leaders he stormed out of the A. F. of L. at the head of his own Committee (later Congress) of Industrial Organizations and for four brawling, bloody years led the confrontation between entrenched management and the aroused workingman. Under him labor revived the sit-down strike, an ancient weapon used at least four centuries earlier by workmen in Rouen Cathedral. A sit-down in the Cleveland Fisher Body plant in Flint, Michigan, in the winter of 1936-37 spread to sixty factories in fourteen states, involved more than 150,000 workers directly or indirectly, and after forty-four days brought giant General Motors to deal with the unions. Later strikes against Chrysler and Ford were also successful.

After the conquest of the auto industry in 1937, everybody expected a really titanic conflict between Lewis and Big Steel, as the United States Steel Company was, and still is, called, in contrast to the four smaller companies usually lumped together as "Little Steel." What actually happened was that Lewis was introduced, in the Mayflower Hotel dining room in Washington, D.C., to Myron Taylor, chairman of the board of Big Steel.

Imperious John L. Lewis ponders a point at a press conference during a 1945 struggle between mine owners and his U.M.W. A strike that year cost the wartime United States economy 13,000,000 tons of soft coal.

a passion equal only to that accorded Franklin Roosevelt, with whom Lewis had one of his most resounding falling-outs.

Early in Roosevelt's regime Lewis and his miners had coughed up $500,000 for an F.D.R. presidential campaign, but Roosevelt lost his temper over the prolonged Little Steel strike and snapped, in conscious parody of the Lewis speaking style, "A plague o' both your houses!" Lewis went on radio to rumble a reply nobody who heard it could ever forget: "It ill behooves one who has supped at labor's table and who has been sheltered in labor's house to curse with equal fervor and fine impartiality both labor and its adversaries when they become locked in deadly embrace."

Wow!

James Caesar Petrillo was less impressive physically than John L. Lewis. He looked like an actor in a gangster movie, swore fluently and was known as the "Mussolini of Music." He was less musical than his brother Caesar James, a trombonist and dance band leader, but great at protecting the rights and privileges of professional, organized musicians.

He first became a power in organized music in Chicago and never relaxed his grip on his beloved Chicago local even after rising to the presidency of the whole American Federation of Musicians. Under Petrillo, as Chicago went, so went the nation. Any benefit he won for Chicago musicians was soon reflected elsewhere. He vastly increased union membership and the average pay of musicians while reducing their working hours. His goal was to make sure that musicians got paid for every note they played and even for some they didn't. He made radio stations pay musicians who had been playing just for the publicity. He eliminated free rehearsals and forbade musicians to engage in public jam sessions. They could play for fun if they wanted to, he said, but people ought to pay to listen. He established the standby rule, which seemed to mean that nobody could make any music in public unless a professional musician was standing by and getting paid, whether he played or not.

His rulings had some odd results. He banned sound trucks from Chicago political campaigns, forcing politicians to use live music or none. When eight Chinese Boy Scouts in Chicago planned to blow a series of bugle blasts to welcome a giant panda to the local zoo, Petrillo insisted that eight professional musicians be engaged for the same event, whether they blew or not.

All through the Swing Era, he fought to get more money for musicians from the sale and use of recordings. To this end he pulled his men out of recording studios for 27 months in 1942-44 and again through most of 1948. These bans helped to popularize singers as against instrumentalists and to speed the demise of the big bands, but musicians, by and large, remained grateful to Petrillo. They kept him in office for years at an annual salary totaling some $46,000 plus various

He asked Taylor for an appointment and called on him next day. Despite his fire-breathing public image, Lewis could be immensely charming. He fascinated Taylor and apparently impressed him with his wide-ranging knowledge of high finance. After a series of meetings Taylor signed a contract with the C.I.O. When the news broke it was like reading a headline saying "Pope Elopes." Then Lewis put his armor back on and led his troops into a temporarily unsuccessful shooting, head-cracking war with Little Steel.

Such minor setbacks hardly impaired the Lewis image. Until his death in 1969 and despite the rise of more streamlined labor leaders like Walter Reuther, Lewis remained for us Swing Era people our favorite incarnation of Big Labor. Certainly organized labor in the U.S. was never the same after his arrival. He was caricatured, maligned, called "czar," hated, loved and followed with extra allowances and showered him with little additional benefits like a car, a chauffeur, bodyguards, a $25,000 summer home and a trip to Europe for himself and his wife. Even corrosive columnist Westbrook Pegler was inspired to speak of J. Caesar as he did of few labor leaders. Petrillo, he said, "is, to my almost certain knowledge and to my strong conviction, not a crook."

Labor leaders like Lewis and Petrillo were the natural enemies of industrialists, but for most of the first decade of the Swing Era, industrialists didn't know whether they were madder at labor or the government. They certainly spent a lot of time being mad at Brigadier General Hugh S. ("Ironpants") Johnson, one of the slew of non-politicians Roosevelt's New Deal brought to Washington to get the economy going again.

Tears for 'Madama Butterfly'

Johnson got his nickname during his early years as a rough, tough cavalry officer. When F.D.R. made him head of the National Recovery Administration he had been out of the Army for fifteen years, working as an aide to financier Bernard Baruch.

As head of the NRA he was supposed to cajole or bully U.S. industry into organizing fair practices codes to regulate wages and prices and to expand employment. Roosevelt had intended to put him in charge also of a huge public works program but changed his mind at the last minute, perhaps because of a comment relayed to him from Baruch: "I think he's a good number-three man, maybe a good number-two man, but he's not a number-one man . . . do tell the President to be careful." Roosevelt gave the public works instead to Secretary of the Interior Harold Ickes, a curmudgeon as sulphurous in his own way as Johnson. Johnson, who was highly emotional for a cavalryman (he used to cry at performances of *Madama Butterfly*) tearfully accepted his truncated responsibilities and a salary of $6,000 a year.

Finding it hard at first to generate enthusiasm for his codes, Johnson designed an NRA symbol — a blue eagle, clutching a cogwheel in one claw and the traditional lightning bolts in the other, above the legend WE DO OUR PART. Business establishments that had signed the President's Re-Employment Agreement or were operating under approved codes were entitled to display the eagle, and patriotic purchasers were supposed to patronize only Blue Eagle firms. Johnson called people who didn't stick to their codes "chisellers" and, to keep the eagle flying, he organized the biggest, loudest, most effective propaganda campaign since World War I. He landed on page one of most newspapers every time he opened his mouth, which he often did. The Blue Eagle showed up not only in store windows but on mastheads of cooperating newspapers and magazines, on highway billboards and in cinemas.

An NRA parade in New York City drew an incredible

At sixty-six inches, dapper James C. Petrillo in 1940 looked every inch a music czar. He sounded like Jimmy Durante impersonating a top sergeant and admitted he was "gettin' a repetition fer bein' a dictator."

250,000 marchers. There were so many people marching that the mere crush of their bodies splintered plate glass windows on 58th Street and upended both a sweating policeman and his frantic horse. When the lights went on at dusk there were people still marching. Theatergoers watched and waved, saw their plays and found more marchers still at it when the curtain went down.

The NRA was a visible sign of the New Deal's efforts

to do something about the Depression, and people were ready to applaud any effort in that direction. Motorcades, brass bands and torchlight processions met Johnson at landing fields when he barnstormed the country plugging NRA. Less entranced were the businessmen who rushed to Washington to seek advice on how to write (or get out of writing) their codes. They got lost in the halls of the Commerce Department, where the NRA had its offices, stood in queues to try to call

A 1934 Chicago *Tribune* cartoon, "Working on his eagle again," attacks Johnson's assumption of vast powers.

General Johnson, and asked each other, "Who is this 'Robbie' who is supposed to be a magic help?" Robbie was redheaded Miss Frances Robinson, secretary to Ironpants, who ushered callers in to see the red-faced, perspiring general at a littered desk, his coat off, his blue shirt open at the neck, waving his arms and bellowing at people or into telephones. (NRA sometimes got 600 phone calls an hour, half of them long distance.) People got worn out just looking at him.

NRA codes were supposed to be voluntary; Johnson got his volunteers the old Army way. He once kept a delegation of steel men sequestered for twelve hours until he had achieved a "voluntary" agreement. He flew off in an Army plane to Detroit to hammer out a trade code for the automobile industry, got it, rushed to Cleveland for a sandwich and a beer. Buttonholed there by a reporter who asked, "What will happen to objectors who don't go along with this new code?" Johnson said, "They'll get a sock right on the nose."

For several heady months it seemed that the NRA was the U.S. government and Hugh Johnson was the NRA, but the old soldier saw ambushes ahead. "The time will come when there won't be so much applause," he said. He plowed ahead, working, it seemed, around the clock, substituting alcohol and cigarettes for sleep and food.

"No member of the government," wrote Arthur Krock after Johnson's first year with the NRA, "the President included, has worked harder or more devotedly for recovery . . . he has shortened his days by the passionate energy with which he has attacked his colossal labor."

The jerry-built structure of NRA, depending as it did more on goodwill than law, began crumbling along with Johnson. By the time he was forced out of the job in October 1934, resigning, as he put it, in "a hail of dead cats," the Blue Eagle was starting to moult. By 1935, the same year the Supreme Court killed NRA, Johnson had recovered enough to become an anti-New Deal columnist who called his former colleagues "economic pansies." He died in 1942 at fifty-nine.

By contrast with Johnson, Alvin A. ("Shipwreck") Kelly was a model of restrained activity. He carved out his niche in thin air, sitting on flagpoles. Kelly's most famous feat was 1,177 hours on a pole on the Steel Pier in Atlantic City in the summer of 1930. His wife ran food and water up to him on a pulley. The plumbing arrangements were never discussed. Kelly occasionally dozed at his post, and he claimed that he kept from falling off his circular, eight-inch seat by thrusting his thumbs into holes like bowling-ball holes in the seat itself. If he started to topple in his sleep, he said, the excruciating pain in his thumbs woke him up.

Kelly was a sailor who was said to have survived five sea disasters, two airplane accidents, three auto accidents and a train wreck. Beyond winning a few bets and getting a little commercial sponsorship, he never made much money flagpole-sitting; between sits he worked as a rigger in the shipyards. He claimed to be a physiculturalist who thought people ate too much and was out to prove that they could get along on as little food as a man could eat while sitting on a flagpole. His name became a household word, but success never dazzled him. He called himself "the biggest fool on earth" but continued perching in the sky until he ran into a spell of bad luck and prejudice. Police in New York dragged him down off the George Washington Bridge one day on the flimsy excuse that they were "preserving his health." They hauled him down from a 65-foot flagpole in front of a Times Square hotel because he was a "traffic menace." Kelly died in 1952, but his nickname lived on for a while in the person of John Simms Kelly, the footballer who was the first husband of socialite Brenda Diana Duff Frazier.

The glitter of a lone green eye

Another skilled practitioner of an unremunerative art was James Leo ("One Eye") Connelly who was born and raised in Lowell, Massachusetts, and began life as a house painter. Then he found his spiritual home in sports. He gave up boxing after losing an eye in what must have been a most unsporting encounter and devoted the next sixty years to amusing himself and the nation by avoiding paying for tickets to anything. Without credentials he walked into football games, baseball games, boxing matches and dogfights. He should have been easy to spot. He was fat, usually unshaven, and he clearly had only one usable eye. But there was something about the green glitter of that remaining eye that seemed to put the whammy on otherwise sensible citizens.

He was a master of the simple, logical disguise. At the Jack Dempsey-Georges Carpentier bout in Jersey City he was repulsed at thirteen of the fifteen entrances to the arena. Then he got into the fourteenth by the simple device of borrowing a pail of coffee and a basket of sandwiches from the telegraph crew on duty. The guards at the fourteenth gate thought he was a vendor. At the 1940 Democratic convention, One Eye walked in the door *carrying* a door that he had surreptitiously removed from a nearby cafe. He had done a similar trick at a boxing match almost twenty years before, carrying eighty pounds of ice.

Andy Frain, boss of an expert band of private protection guards, called Connelly "a genius." Frain said

During National Doughnut Week, flagpole sitter Shipwreck Kelly dunked thirteen doughnuts on Friday, October 13, 1939 while standing on his head on a plank thrust out of a 54th-story window of New York's Chanin Building. He said he did it to combat superstition.

he once gave a special briefing to all of his guards at a political convention to keep Connelly out. "When I went into the hall," reported Frain ruefully, "there he was, in the middle of the floor, selling ice water to the delegates at fifty cents a glass."

During World War II Connelly accepted an appointment from the self-styled King of the Hobos to head a hobo constabulary aimed at stamping out "fifth-column stuff" in the U.S. By war's end he had matured so much he actually took a job as a legitimate usher during a World Series at Chicago's Wrigley Field. Trained for years to know a phony when he saw one, Usher Connelly stopped a man who looked okay but who was headed for one of the choice, expensive, box seats.

"Who are you?" Connelly asked.

"I'm P. K. Wrigley Jr., owner of the Chicago Cubs," said the man.

"That's for the birds," said One Eye Connelly. The man was who he said he was, and Connelly was fired on the spot.

How to get a job on horseback

Samuel Hoffenstein, a poet of the Swing Era, once complained about the tedium of getting dressed every day only to get undressed again. Sally Rand couldn't have agreed less. She didn't invent the striptease — that goes back at least to Salome and her seven veils — but she made her name synonymous with the art of fandancing. It took her a while to work down to basics. She started out as a self-styled acrobatic dancer from Missouri and tried nightclubs, movies, touring shows and selling yachts to rumrunners on commission, all with limited success. In 1933 she was trying to think up a new number for her act in a Chicago nightclub. Gypsy Rose Lee and Ann Corio, among others, were doing all right in burlesque houses at the time, peeling off evening gowns and the like, but nobody was doing much with fans. The success of Sally's new act inspired her to a stroke of genius. She rented a white horse and a trailer and trundled off to a yacht where Mrs. William Randolph Hearst was giving a high-society dinner for the benefit of the Milk Fund. Gloriously undressed as Lady Godiva, Sally rode up the gangplank before the dazzled eyes of the assembled press. The next day she landed a job as a fan dancer in the Streets of Paris show at the just-opened Century of Progress fair.

Thirty-nine million people attended the fair, and though not all of them admitted they went there primarily to see Sally, it is a fact that she remained profitably in business ever after. Even ostriches never handled their plumes as deftly as Sally. She has said that after she started fan-dancing she was never out of work for more than four months at a time. "I worked hard," she once remarked, "but I never made any money until I took my pants off."

The same city that launched Sally Rand also pro-

"There is a science in gate-crashing," said its greatest practitioner, One Eye Connelly, "just as there is in everything else." Here he scouts the Rose Bowl prior to crashing the 1931 New Year's Day football game.

duced the Swing Era's most improbable athlete, Harry Krakow, better known as "King Levinsky." The King, a former fish peddler, beat a whole bunch of prizefighting bums fairly easily, and once he even managed to outpoint the skillful Tommy Loughran. But he was known more for his assaults on the English language than for any damage he inflicted on other boxers. "It don't feel like nuttin'," he said when sports writer Paul Gallico asked him what it was like to be hit on the chin by Joe Louis, but admitted that for a while afterwards he was "in a transom." He once blamed a loss to Irish crooner Jack Doyle on the debilitating effects of the British climate and a surfeit of tea. "It was 'Cheerio' here and 'Cheerio' there, and tea until it ran out your ears," complained King Levinsky. "Before the fight I was rarin' to go, and then they postponed it. I was over-trained on it all."

On that same ill-starred trip, Levinsky attended a press luncheon in London at which the toastmaster arose, lifted his glass and said, "Gentlemen, the King." You know what that Levinsky did? He got up and took a bow, that's what he did.

In 1938, eleven years after Charles Lindbergh flew solo from New York to Paris and one year after tousle-haired Amelia Earhart, who had set international flying records galore, vanished with her navigator on the Pacific leg of a daring round-the-world flight, Douglas Corrigan, a thirty-one-year-old airplane mechanic in Inglewood, California, took it into his head to fly to Paris. He owned an ancient, gummed-together Curtiss-Robin monoplane which he had bought six years before at an auction. He had paid $900 for it and he called it *Lizzie*. He also had a brown leather jacket, *de rigeur* for intrepid airmen of the day, and a lot of nerve. Some of his friends and fellow pilots were dubious about his project, but Corrigan took off anyway and got *Lizzie* all the way from California to New York, a triumph that went largely unnoticed because at the same time Howard Hughes was making a spectacular three-day flight around the world.

In New York City the Bureau of Air Commerce turned down Corrigan's plan to fly to Paris. His plane, they said, had no safety devices and no radio. Even worse, Corrigan had added so many extra gas tanks that he had to fly the thing looking out the side windows.

Sally Rand and a horse do a 1937 reprise of the Lady Godiva act that launched her career at Chicago's 1933 Century of Progress Exposition. A lady lawyer complained about Sally's fan dance there, but a bored judge ruled that if "a lot of boobs come to see a woman wiggle with a fan . . . we have a right to cater to them."

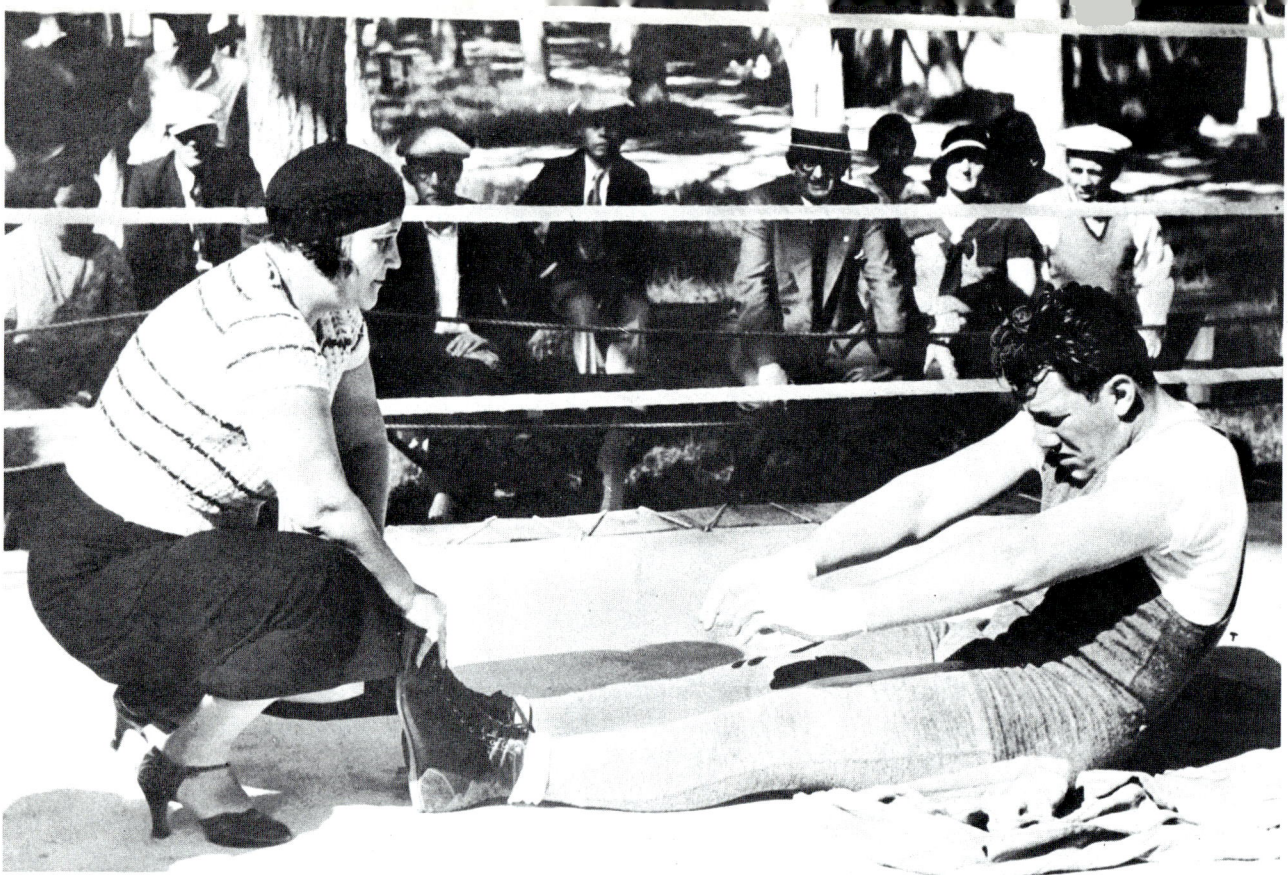

Boxer "King" Levinsky trains under the stern eye of his sister, Mrs. Lena Levy, better known as "Leaping Lena." She managed Levinsky, sparred with him on the rare occasions when he sparred at all, terrified other managers into giving him bouts, and made him one of the best paid, if least able, fisticuffers of his time.

The bureau's carefully studied opinion was that trying to fly to Paris in it was tantamount to suicide.

On a July morning in 1938 Corrigan climbed into *Lizzie*, arranged his Irish features into an appropriate mask of sorrow at the collapse of his dreams, bade farewell to the manager of Floyd Bennett Field in New York City, and took off, ostensibly for California. His provisions consisted of two boxes of fig biscuits, some chocolate bars, a bottle of water and fifteen dollars in cash.

Just over twenty-eight hours later he landed at Baldonnel Airport in Dublin, Ireland. Airport officials surveyed his aircraft with wonder and opined that it might possibly have been blown in from some nearby place like Shannon. "I've just flown from New York," said the bleary pilot. "Where am I?" They told him. "I intended," said Corrigan with a completely straight face, "to fly to California."

"Wrong Way" Corrigan never retracted his story that *Lizzie's* compass had got stuck and led him into a simple navigational error. Perhaps his limited view from the cockpit prevented him from noticing that there was an awful lot of ocean between New York and California. The United States ambassador in London, Joseph P. Kennedy, congratulated Corrigan on his coup and America welcomed him home with a ticker-tape procession down Fifth Avenue.

"Your deliberate impetuosity," said Mayor Fiorello La Guardia, "your Pickwickian impulsiveness, naturally finds a responsive chord in me."

Another celebrated flier of the time sported a sky-blue uniform, a kepi and silver spurs. This pilot's business card read, "Colonel Hubert Fauntleroy Julian, M.D., World's Greatest Parachute Jumper." He was the Black Eagle of Harlem, a man of colossal gall and courage.

Emperor Haile Selassie of Ethiopia once impulsively named Hubert Julian the commander in chief of the Abyssinian air force — two Junker monoplanes left over from World War I and a dainty Gipsy Moth, purchased from Selfridge's Department Store in London. Colonel Julian flew the Junkers very well and even taught some Ethiopians to fly them. Then he blew it all on the occasion of the Emperor's coronation.

A falling leaf that kept on falling

Haile Selassie wanted nothing to mar this perfect day. The lovely little Gipsy Moth wasn't even to be flown but merely to be displayed on the airfield. Colonel Julian just couldn't abide this thought. Such a beautiful plane had to be flown. At a coronation rehearsal he impulsively rushed onto the airfield, climbed into the Moth and took off. He flew twice around the field, banked, waggled his wings at the Emperor, and then put the plane into a maneuver that pilots of the time called a "falling leaf." Obeying some law of nature beyond the ken of the colonel, the Moth kept falling. The motor failed and both of the Emperor's favorites, the plane and the pilot, landed in an untidy heap almost at his feet.

Helpful hands lifted Julian from the wreckage. One punishment for defying the Emperor was summary removal of the offender's hands and feet. Perhaps because of the presence of an eminent relative of the King of England, Julian was simply handed his passport and sent home. He arrived in New York sporting a monocle and a British accent, assuring reporters that he had been sabotaged by jealous French pilots who before his advent had been very important in the Ethiopian court.

Colonel Julian was born in Trinidad and made his way to the U.S. via Canada. He had a passion for flying and he showed up in the Jersey Palisades in the early '20s professing to be a parachute jumper who needed practice. Pilot Clarence Chamberlin, an early transatlantic flier, loaned him a parachute and took him aloft but found the colonel oddly reluctant to jump. In the end Chamberlin just plain shook Julian off the wings of the biplane at about 3,000 feet. Julian was so reluctant even then to jump that he took one of the plane's wing-struts with him, clutched firmly in one hand. Chamberlin landed the remainder of his airplane with some difficulty and then ran to look for his passenger. Julian was safely on earth, uncomfortably tangled in the parachute shroudlines but irrepressible. "That," said he, "was certainly my most remarkable jump."

After that he really did learn to jump and he learned to fly. He made some spectacular leaps over Harlem, jumping just for joy or for pay from any entrepreneur who could afford him. Vagrant winds once blew him through the window of a police station and another time deposited him on top of a schoolhouse spire. He developed something he called the Saxophonerparachutta-preresistationist. Got it? It was a motor-driven parachute that freed both his hands and his attention so he could play airs on a saxophone while drifting earthward. Once he took up a collection of small change in Harlem and made his first seaplane flight, headed "non-stop to Addis Ababa, in Abyssinia." He flew a few hundred yards and crash-landed in Flushing Bay.

He went back to Ethiopia one more time after the Gipsy Moth debacle because he felt he should help Haile Selassie fight the Italian invaders. He was rebuffed, however, and in 1935 he announced he had come to the "unanimous conclusion" that Ethiopia neither wanted nor deserved his help. "Your Supreme Illustriousness," he said in his farewell to the Emperor, "it is with overflowing emotion and bleeding heart that I am resigning as an officer of the great army of the conquer-

Colonel Hubert Fauntleroy Julian, "Black Eagle of Harlem" (*above, center*), set a snappy example in 1935 for Ethiopian troops awaiting Italian invasion, but as he had in 1930, when he crashed Haile Selassie's pet plane during coronation rehearsal, he soon left the country.

Dauntless Douglas Corrigan stands beside the plane he flew the "wrong way" to Ireland in 1938. The value to aviation of his daring flight was nil, but he earned $85,000 from personal appearances and other fruits of fame as well as lifetime membership in a Liars Club.

ing Lion of Judah." He turned up shortly afterward in Italy, claiming to be an Italian citizen "by conquest."

He volunteered to fly for Finland in that little nation's hopeless war against the Soviet Union. He rushed off by ship, arrived twenty-four days after hostilities ended and came home with an impressive Finnish uniform. Then he volunteered for Britain's Royal Air Force, was briefly accepted, and loudly challenged Germany's Air Marshal Hermann Goering to a man-to-man dogfight at 10,000 feet over the Channel. Goering never replied. In the end Julian enlisted in the U.S. Army and spent two years as an Air Corps sergeant in World War II.

In the '50s and '60s he kept busy selling arms to a variety of customers from the Caribbean to the Congo, had his passport lifted once by the U.S. government and spent four months in jail on suspicion of being a mercenary in Katanga Province. He said he was just supplying doctors and medical supplies to his old friend Moise Tshombe.

Throughout most of World War II, the European theater attracted the most attention and got most of the newspaper space. Two reasons for this were a couple of wiry little men, Bill Mauldin and Ernie Pyle.

Willie: "Joe, yestiddy ya saved my life an' I swore I'd pay ya back. Here's my last pair of dry socks."

Among enlisted men, his favorite subjects, correspondent Ernie Pyle (*center*) listens to war news aboard a transport carrying him toward Okinawa and death.

Ernie Pyle weighed 110 pounds and was getting bald. He didn't look like a hero, he just was one. He had been a newspaperman for seventeen years and was a highly successful syndicated columnist when he went to Britain in 1940 to cover the blitz. During his few remaining years he was never far from front-line troops and violent death. He covered the landings in North Africa, Sicily, Anzio and Normandy. He knew General "Ike" Eisenhower and he respected him, but he didn't write much about him. Ernie Pyle knew that "war to an individual is hardly ever bigger than a hundred yards on either side of him" and that's what he wrote about. He wrote about the hundred yards and the mud and the terror. He wrote about letters from home and young men who sometimes cried; about the simple agony of injustice that wars can't correct; about humor and cruelty and compassion. He wrote simply and vividly, and the papers that carried Ernie Pyle's words reached more than thirteen million readers a week. Most soldiers would rather have been mentioned in Ernie's column than in an official citation.

One of his most celebrated columns described some infantrymen in Italy saying goodby to their commanding officer who had been killed in combat:

"One soldier came and looked down and he said out loud, 'God damn it!' That's all he said, and then he walked away . . . another man came, I think he was an officer. It was hard to tell officers from men in the half

Driving his personal jeep, Bill Mauldin, creator of *Willie and Joe*, slithers through Italian mud in 1945 as he advances with U.S. 5th Army in World War II.

Another war, another generation; Bill Mauldin (*right*) visits his son, Warrant Officer Bruce P. Mauldin, a helicopter pilot, at Pleiku, South Vietnam, in 1965.

light for all were bearded and grimy dirty. The man looked down into the dead captain's face, and then he spoke directly to him, as though he were alive. He said: 'I'm sorry, old man.'

"Then a soldier came and stood beside the officer and bent over and he, too, spoke to his dead captain, not in a whisper, but awfully tenderly, and he said, 'I sure am sorry, sir.'

"Then the first man squatted down and he reached down and took the dead hand and he sat there for five full minutes, holding the dead hand in his own and looking intently into the dead face and he never uttered a sound all the time he sat there. And then finally he put the hand down, and then reached up and gently straightened the points of the captain's shirt collar, and then he sort of arranged the tattered edges of his uniform around the wound. And then he got up and walked away down the road in the moonlight all alone."

Late in 1944 Pyle came back to the U.S. and permitted himself to be lionized by the home folks for about three months. Then he couldn't stand it any more. "I've

Sergeant Charles E. ("Commando") Kelly waves from his modest Pittsburgh, Pennsylvania, home in 1944 after returning, much decorated, from Italy. The stars on the sign symbolize Kelly and his six brothers, all in service.

got to go — and I hate it," he told his wife. On the tiny island of Ie Shima, just off Okinawa, a Japanese machine gunner got him. He hadn't been in the Pacific long, but the GIs there knew who he was and what he was. They buried him with their own dead, and when the war was over they named a movie house for him in occupied Tokyo.

The GIs also loved Bill Mauldin for his portrayal of the real, unvarnished, untidy soldier. Mauldin was a scrawny, eighteen-year-old Army truck driver when he got a chance to draw cartoons for his division's newspaper. His illustrations of barracks humor soon crystallized around two infantrymen, Willie and Joe, as immortal as the Good Soldier Schweik. They were grimy, amoral, bedraggled, indomitable. They still come to life on the page as they sit in a foxhole growling at each other, "Why the hell couldn't you have been born a beautiful woman?" Willie saves Joe's life; Joe repays him with his last pair of dry socks. "Just gimme a coupla aspirin," says Willie to the medical corpsman offering him a medal. "I already got a Purple Heart."

Mauldin's pen often punctured high-ranking pomposity. "What a beautiful view," says a fatuous officer. "Is there one for the enlisted men?" Cartoons like that irked some brass; General George Patton tried vainly to get Mauldin to smarten up his characters. Mauldin remained unrepentant and won a Pulitzer Prize for cartooning. He took Willie and Joe back into civilian life with him. They all had some trouble adjusting; Willie and Joe, in fact, expired, but Mauldin recovered beautifully and became one of his country's half-dozen best political cartoonists.

Outlaw instincts and burglar's guts

Few of that war's heroes equaled the record of "Commando" Kelly, a twenty-three-year-old infantryman with the instincts of an outlaw and the guts of a second-story man. He was a thin-faced, red-haired technical sergeant from Pittsburgh who had been christened Charles E. Kelly. He wound up in Italy where he won the nation's highest award, the Congressional Medal of Honor. In September 1943, Kelly volunteered to join a patrol whose mission was to wipe out some German machine-gun positions. After the patrol accomplished this, Kelly volunteered again to report the victory to battalion headquarters. Headquarters had moved, however, and after Kelly had walked, crawled, and run through fire looking for it, he felt impelled to go back to the patrol and report the move. He landed smack in the middle of another shooting match between the patrol and some well-entrenched Germans. Ammunition was low and Kelly volunteered again to go get supplies. He returned to the fray. "We were in a three-story building," he said later. "When the third floor got too hot we

moved to the second. When that got too hot we went to the first, then back to the third again. I burned out four automatic rifles, they got so hot."

Happening upon some sixty-millimeter mortar shells, Kelly conceived the idea of pulling the safety pins on these sensitive projectiles and then using them as outsized hand grenades. This activity amused him for some time, but eventually the position became untenable and the patrol slipped away. Kelly remained behind to cover the retreat. His weapon at this moment was a bazooka, which he methodically loaded and fired until he ran out of shells. Then, on his way back home to bed, Kelly found an antitank gun that nobody seemed to be using, so he loitered long enough to fire

An unparalleled welcome greeted General Dwight D. Eisenhower on his return, victorious, from Europe in

all its shells at the advancing enemy. That done, he found his company and reported in. He was officially credited with having wiped out forty Nazis in twenty-four hours. Welcomed home to Pittsburgh as a hero, he told everybody that the whole idea of heroism was "the bunk," then promptly went AWOL from a job as an infantry instructor at Fort Benning, Georgia.

The war ended, and the most popular man in the U.S., possibly in the world, was Dwight David Eisenhower from Abilene, Kansas. He had led the successful Allied invasion of the continent and the defeat of Hitler's Germany. He had captured reticent British hearts by turning up in London after the victory and expressing his delight at being "back in a country whose language I almost speak." He had made his lopsided grin and his sawed-off military jacket part of the nation's folklore, and like all other triumphant survivors he went home to be feted. There was a week-long celebration in Abilene in 1945, and everybody from old pals to old pols hailed Ike Eisenhower as "our next President." Ike just grinned, and shuffled his feet, and finally he answered them.

"There's no use denying that I'll fly to the moon," he said, "because I couldn't if I wanted to. The same goes for politics."

Nobody noticed it at the time, but that was a watershed remark. That was the end of an era.

—DORA JANE HAMBLIN

July 1945. More than 1,000,000 people cheered him in Washington. Here a motor cavalcade carries Ike and his staff through a whirl of paper and cloth in New York's garment district, part of a thirty-seven-mile triumph.

The Men Who Made the Music:
Lionel Hampton

Lionel Hampton comes on strong at the National Theater of the Palais de Chaillot in Paris on his first trip abroad in 1953. The Vibes President of the United States, to use one of his cornier titles, was wildly received on this 30-day tour of Europe's top music halls. He has since created the same kind of excitement on every other continent.

One January evening in 1971, long after the Swing Era is generally believed to have ended, the crowd in the stylish Hong Kong Bar of the Century Plaza Hotel in Los Angeles exploded. The detonator was Lionel Hampton. He started the eruption by whaling away at the drums, tossing his sticks and holding extras in each hand, under each arm and under his chin. Then he sang, bobbing his huge shoulders and beaming as he gruffly belted out *My Love Is Like a Seesaw*. He leaped to the vibes and, with head back, eyes closed and tongue between his teeth, played an infinitely tender *Close to You*. He got the audience to join him in singing and clapping out the rhythm of *Hey-Bob-a-Re-Bop*, then led his eight-piece band out onto the floor, intoning, "Heyeyeyaaaahaaahaaa!" and beating out with his drumsticks on one table after another the rhythm of *When the Saints Go Marching In*. Hands reached for him, people jumped up and shouted, "Bravo!" and "More!"

"We're jus' getting warm," Hamp told them. He played a swinging *Aquarius* and a poignant *Yesterdays* and then it was *Flying Home* and the crowd almost blew the Hong Kong Bar apart.

"You keep doing that and you'll have us killing ourselves," he told the crowd, but after being in almost perpetual motion for perhaps sixty-two years, Hamp looked good for another few decades.

Lionel Hampton was born in Birmingham, Alabama, or maybe it was Louisville, Kentucky, in 1909 or perhaps 1913 or 1914. Records are missing or inconclusive, and Hamp is vague on details. During the First World War, his father Charles, a pianist and singer, was listed as missing in action. His mother took Lionel to live with her parents, who soon moved to Chicago "when all the blacks," as Hamp says, "were moving North—to get freedom."

"I was raised by the women in my family. They were all good people who had jobs and kept a clean house. My grandmother set the tone for the family. She was between the Holy Rollers and the hard-shell Baptists. She brought me up to believe in the Bible. She believed in faith healing and the power of prayer. We never had medicine in our house as long as my grandmother lived."

Chicago in the '20s was full of jazz and crime. "Because of the youth gangs and crime, I was sent to private [parochial] schools. That's where I learned drums. I always

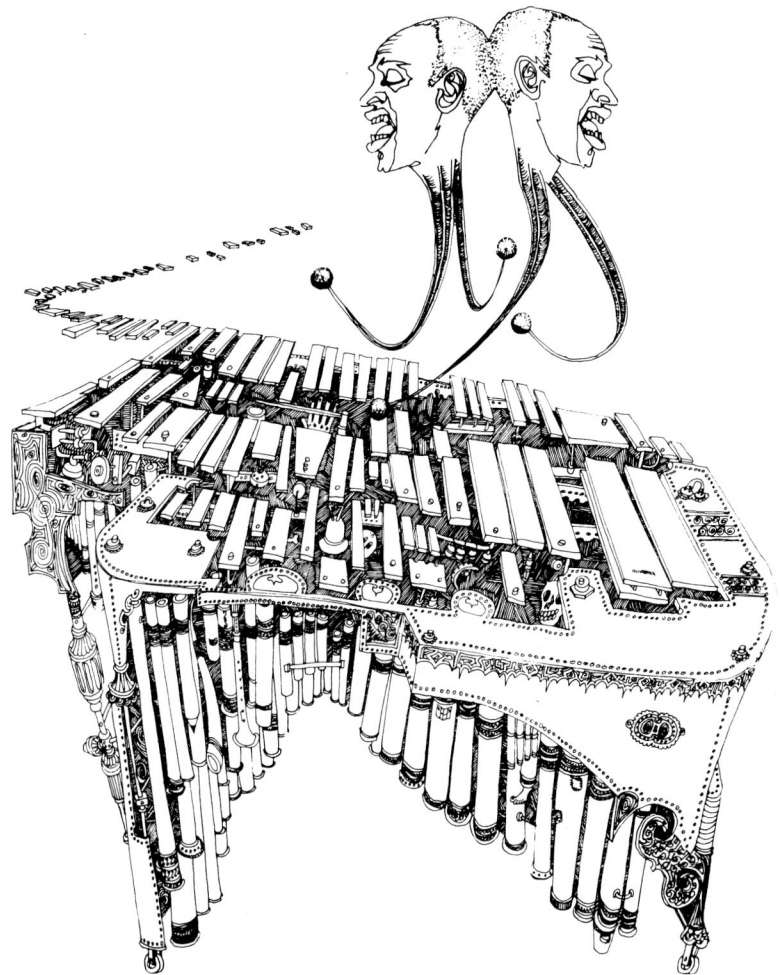

wanted to be a drummer. Sister Peters—I think that was her name—gave me drum lessons. She learned me the real way—all the rudiments. She cracked me on the knuckles when I didn't get it right."

Lionel was a lively boy who stuttered, as he still does, when excited. He was rough on drums. "I'd get two or three drums for Christmas and have them all broken by New Year's." With one finger of each hand—the style he still uses—he banged out on the family piano his school music and, oftener, solos copied from Louis Armstrong and Earl Hines. He joined a boys' band sponsored by the Negro newspaper, the *Chicago Defender*. He began as bass drum carrier but soon rose to beating the big drum and then to playing the snare in the marching band and tympani in the concert band.

"They brought in a great teacher—Major N. Clark

Hampton sits in the middle of Les Hite's band, just in front of the tuba. The sidemen are inside what is supposed to be a watermelon rind, part of a set for the 1932 movie *Taxi!*, one of several films in which the Hite band appeared. Hite *(fore-ground)* started his band with some of the youngsters who had played with him in Paul Howard's Quality Serenaders. In addition to Hampton, Hite's bands included at various times trumpeters Louis Armstrong and Dizzy Gillespie.

Smith. He'd been with Teddy Roosevelt's Rough Riders. I had to learn all the percussion instruments, including xylophone. And we learned harmony from him. We learned about flatted fifths and all that stuff modern guys play." The band marched in parades and won honors in competitions. Lionel found he enjoyed success and applause.

He also enjoyed the jazz he heard at the Grand Terrace Ballroom, the Sunset Cafe and the Vendome Theater. "We'd peek in the windows of the Grand Terrace. We lived near the Sunset on the South Side of Chicago, and in summer some of us kids used to sneak in the back door to hear Louis." Louis Armstrong was also sitting in with the fifteen-piece Erskine Tate band at the Vendome. Lionel followed him there and watched drummer Jimmy Bertrand tossing his sticks and leaping up to play the xylophone or the chimes, as lights winked inside the big bass drum. Hamp took some lessons from Bertrand, who taught many of the Chicago drummers of the time, and persuaded his uncle to buy him a xylophone.

Hampton's grandmother died, and in 1928 he moved with his aunt to Los Angeles where he jobbed around for two years with minor-league outfits like the Spikes Brothers and Paul Howard's Quality Serenaders. Another sideman in those bands was Les Hite, a Chicago saxophonist who

decided to form his own group. Hite hired Hamp and some other teen-agers, indoctrinated his young band with Fletcher Henderson, Duke Ellington and Don Redman records and got a job at Sebastian's Cotton Club in Culver City. "That's where all the movie stars went," says Hamp.

Louis Armstrong turned up at the Cotton Club as a soloist, then fronted the Hite band at the club and on records for the OKeh label. During a break at a recording session, Hampton started riffing on some vibes he found in the studio. "Sounds good, do it on records," Hamp remembers Armstrong's saying. So Hamp added a touch of vibes to *Memories of You* and did the same thing, five months later, in *Just a Gigolo*.

All drummers are said to yearn for more melodic instruments. Hamp still played drums in Les Hite's band, but he learned also to play chords on a set of bells the band's pianist owned; he kept hammering out melodies on the piano with his two forefingers, and he kept exploring his new instrument, the vibes.

His xylophone training helped, but nobody could teach him much about vibes because nobody knew much. The "vibraharp" was a 1927 refinement of the slightly earlier "vibraphone"—the name most people still attach to the instrument. Both are cousins of the xylophone, but have metal instead of wooden tone bars. The vibraharp has a resonator beneath each tone bar. Inside each resonator is a little disc attached to a rod which runs through all the resonators. An electric motor rotates the rod; the whirling discs give each note the vibrato for which the instrument

is named. A foot pedal permits the player to damp the resonators.

The obstacles confronting an aspiring vibes man are considerable. A good instrument like Hampton's costs $2,000 and weighs about 200 pounds. The player is at one remove from his instrument because he uses mallets instead of his mouth or his fingers. He uses his wrists and elbows even more than a pianist does and has trouble making himself heard in a big band.

Hamp was the first jazz musician to feature the vibes. Hite had no use for vibes in his band; he wanted Hamp to stick to drums. But Frank Sebastian, who owned the Cotton Club, liked Hamp's vibes and kept him on after Hite left the club in 1934. Gladys Riddle encouraged Lionel, too. She was a part-Indian girl from Oklahoma whose mother ran a Los Angeles hotel. "Gladys was a modiste," Hamp says. "Sewed for the stars—Marion Davies, Norma Shearer, Joan Crawford. She was making all that money. I was going with her, and she gave me vibes for my birthday." She also encouraged him to study music at the University of Southern California, "but I didn't finish."

A mortgage to keep the band going

With Buck Clayton and others, Hamp played at the Cotton Club and then, with a band that included Herschel Evans ("Boy, could he play tenor!") toured up and down the Coast. "The agents took off with all the money, so Gladys mortgaged her mother's house to keep the band going."

The band wound up in the Paradise Cafe, a noisy dive on South Main Street in Los Angeles, usually full of sailors from nearby naval establishments. That tireless jazz scout John Hammond turned up there in 1936 with Harry Goodman, bass player in his brother Benny's band. "He took me there to hear Lionel on the vibes," says Hammond. "I knew about Lionel as a drummer with Les Hite, but this was the first time I'd seen him in the flesh. He had a pretty good little nine-piece band, and as usual he was doing everything."

Hammond brought Benny, who was fascinated by the hyperactive Hampton. The next night Benny reappeared with the rest of the new Goodman trio—drummer Gene Krupa and pianist Teddy Wilson.

"We jammed two hours straight," says Hampton. "Benny said for me to come and make records with him. We went to the Victor studios and made *Moon Glow* and *Dinah*."

On these first records with Goodman, Hampton's solos, backgrounds and "breaks" glow and ring with strong jazz accents—his ideas moving in a dynamic yet orderly flow. With his catchy, fast-moving, four-bar introduction on *Dinah*, he set a beat and a style he has maintained ever since—immediately communicative, swinging and happy.

Within six weeks Goodman wired Hampton to come to New York and make the trio a quartet. Hamp thought it was a joke. Then a railroad ticket arrived. Hamp yelled for Gladys. "You gotta come with me, talk for me." Not without a wedding, said Mrs. Riddle.

Hamp cashed in the railroad ticket and bought a jalopy. He and Gladys stopped first in Yuma, Arizona, across the California border, where they were married on November

Three quarters of a famous four are in this 1937 picture in New York's Madhattan Room. Gene Krupa is on drums, Benny on clarinet and Hamp on vibes. The fourth man was pianist Teddy Wilson. "What he can do," said Goodman of Hampton, "is something nobody else has even approached."

11, 1936, and began a 35-year partnership ended only by Gladys's death in 1971. In New York, Goodman hired them both—Hamp to play in the Madhattan Room of the Pennsylvania Hotel and Gladys to get him to the job on time.

The excitement Hamp generated, his extraordinary musicianship and electric enthusiasm brought him instant success. He pleased both crowds and musicians. "He could talk harmony like a college professor," says a former sideman. His hot and sweet solos added a touch of liquid fire

Hamp was the first U.S. jazzman to take a band to Israel, in 1955. Chief Rabbi Herzog capped him with a *kipah*, taught him some Hebrew and took him to visit King David's tomb.

to the quartet numbers, and his vibes always provided exactly the right notes, chords and riffs to support the clarinet and piano.

A *New Yorker* critic described Hampton in action with the Goodman quartet at the Madhattan Room in 1937: "Benny starts a duel, splitting a hot chorus with Hampton. He plays a few bars, Hampton plinks out some phrases in keeping with the mood set by the clarinet; Benny, enraptured, smiles and has another short say; Hampton, going out of the world, carries on . . ."

The Goodman quartet "carried on" all over the nation. Hampton shrugs off the perils of touring the South as part of a pioneer experiment in integrated music. "We didn't have much trouble. Oh, the cats backstage called Teddy and me 'water boy' sometimes." But in one town police were stationed to keep Wilson and Hampton off the stage; swing fans brushed the cops aside and the concert proceeded. In another, Hamp had a six-policeman escort to the bandstand because of a fracas the night before. Whatever the climate, Hamp usually captivated the crowd once he got going.

While with Goodman, Hampton also led a series of jazz groups in recording sessions that included an astonishing number of topflight musicians. Coleman Hawkins, Benny Carter, Chu Berry and Ben Webster were his "million dollar" sax section in *One Sweet Letter from You*. Johnny Hodges made *On the Sunny Side of the Street* one of his greatest performances. Others who played with Hamp included Harry James, John Kirby, Nat Cole, Ziggy Elman, Cootie Williams, Big Sid Catlett, Cozy Cole and Charlie Christian. They made classics like *Whoa Babe, Jivin' the Vibres* and *Sweethearts on Parade*, one of the jumpingest records of all time. They also made the first of many recordings of Hamp's soaring theme song, *Flying Home*.

In Rome after the 1968 San Remo Song Festival, Hamp and Louis Armstrong were received by Pope Paul VI *(below)*. They gave the Pope a Festival record and some Michelan-

gelo engravings. "Let's get out of here," whispered Armstrong uneasily. "I'm a Baptist. I don't belong here." Hamp, who is deeply if eclectically religious, felt right at home.

On these records Hamp plays vibes, sometimes drums frenetically, occasionally sings with fine rhythm and sincerity if not in one of the century's great voices. These 48 Victor records define beautifully his chief contribution to swing—he makes it sound like fun. He is a consummate showman and, within his limits, a flashy and exciting drummer. His contagious enthusiasm shakes other musicians out of their inhibitions, and his music, whether he calls it swing or boogie or bop, usually comes across like a double helping of joy.

Jess Stacy, who also played piano with Goodman, made several of the Victor sides. "It was fun working with Lionel. Everybody relaxes around him. He certainly had a lot of fine piano players to choose from, and I was honored that he chose me. All musicians respected Lionel as a musician and a leader."

When Goodman fell ill in July 1940 and disbanded his orchestra on the Coast, Lionel decided to strike out with his own band again. One of the first sidemen he recruited was Jean Baptiste Illinois Jacquet, a Louisiana-born, Houston-raised alto player who was jamming around Los Angeles. One night Jacquet's friend Nat King Cole invited Illinois to sit in with the Cole trio and Hampton at Hollywood's Radio Room.

"Hamp played so much that night his vibes fell off the stage," recalls Jacquet. "Afterwards he said to me, 'I want you for my band. But I want you to play on tenor what you're playing on alto.' He's so gifted, he hears right. He knew I should play tenor." Jacquet's tenor solos, according to critic Leonard Feather, "started a whole new school of big-toned, extrovert, erotic tenor sax stylists."

By October Hamp had a band. After bubbling over with "an idea a day," like having the King Cole Trio for a rhythm section, he eventually settled on a band of talented and mostly unknown youngsters. He set the band's style by having the solos from his small-group recordings re-scored for orchestra. Clarinetist Marshal Royal became the band's musical director and led the first (and only) week of rehearsals before the band hit the road.

"The band rehearsed day and night," says Jacquet, "right through my birthday, October 31. We rehearsed so much my lips were all stiff and chapped; when I touched them they felt like rocks. All of a sudden it was November sixth."

The Lionel Hampton Orchestra played its first engagement on November 6, 1940, in the Club Alabam in Los Angeles, then took to the road in a decrepit bus. Gladys had persuaded Joe Glaser's Associated Booking Corporation to advance Hamp ten thousand dollars to start the band; Hamp had blown all but seventy-five of it on a diamond ring and a mink coat for Gladys. Hamp doesn't remember too much about the early band days, but Illinois Jacquet does.

"Our first big jump from California was to Fort Worth, the Hotel Texas. We played every stop, you name it. And Hamp would call rehearsal every day—a couple of hours before the dance in every town. Norfolk, Virginia, was our last stop before New York."

The musicians had no job in New York—they just wanted to see the sights. "We got to the George Washington Bridge, but our raggedy bus couldn't make it into the

Hamp has played at six Presidential inaugurations, starting with Truman's. Here, he attends Eisenhower's first with Guy Lombardo and with his wife, Gladys, whom he married in 1936. She has described her marriage as "like having a husband, child and partner all wrapped up in one person."

city. So we had to unload it, take everything out—our instruments, our luggage. And at the time we didn't have the best luggage. Some of the boys were carrying their mothers' black hat bags. It was my first time in New York. I could see the Empire State Building. But we were still in New Jersey, couldn't get across the bridge. They sent for another bus and we made it into the city—checked in at the fabulous, beautiful Y.M.C.A."

After some sight-seeing, the band took off for Chicago and an engagement at the Grand Terrace, long the stronghold of the formidable Earl Hines band. The men nearly froze in the unheated bus, and the day they hit Chicago, in January 1941, a blizzard dumped fourteen inches of snow on the city. "The wind split my California topcoat right in two," says Jacquet.

A smash at the Grand Terrace

Hamp started rehearsing the band the minute they got off the bus, and they opened at the Grand Terrace that night. "I think the date was originally for a week," says Hamp. "We were such a big success it was extended to a month. After the Grand Terrace we went into the Hotel Sherman. We had air time there and at the Grand Terrace —every night. That was a big boost for the band."

The band gained polish and strength in Chicago. By the time of its next big engagement, at New York's Apollo Theater, it had gained two new sidemen: trumpeter Joe Newman from Montgomery, Alabama, and pianist Milt Buckner, a great "locked hands" piano stylist.

After a two-week smash at the Apollo, it was back to the bus for more one-nighters. "Jacquet would always sit near the front with Karl George, the trumpet player," says Buckner. "They wore riding habits and were the high-lifers. I rode with the low-lifers in the back. Gladys rode in a car

Hampton parades down the aisle of a U.S. theater to the strains of *When the Saints Go Marching In.* The first person to get excited at a Hampton performance is usually Hamp.

Sidemen soon catch the Hampton spirit. At a British music hall Lionel inspires saxophonist Monty Shaw to deliver a horizontal performance during a rendition of *Flying Home.*

ahead of the bus. Hamp didn't like to ride in a car; he liked the bus. Hamp always stayed hungry. We called him 'Shopping Bag.' We'd pass a market or a store and he'd say, 'St-st-stop the bus!" Gladys never gave him any money, so the band would chip in for food. He'd get out and buy himself five, ten dollars' worth of food, and that's when food was cheaper. He'd buy it and eat it all himself. Oh, he offered some around to his favorites."

Hamp says he spends money freely "if I get ahold to it," and most of his former sidemen agree that he became—and stayed—rich largely because Gladys always minded his money. She also handled the sidemen's money, to the dissatisfaction of some. "If I wanted to borrow on my salary," said one, "I'd have to pay interest. It would be six dollars for five, twelve dollars for ten. I was against that. After all, I was only drawing my own money."

The band struggled through the South, playing dance after dance in tobacco warehouses, as struggling black bands still do. "Sometimes the tobacco warehouses were bigger than the towns," says Jacquet. "We'd even be sitting on top of the tobacco." In one paper-mill town the acid in the air bleached the blue stripes on their tuxedo trousers. And they encountered the usual difficulties of black bands in the South trying to find places to eat and sleep.

"In those days," says Marshal Royal, "when you did one-night stands with a black band, you were half beat from the beginning. You couldn't get decent accommodations, there was no place to eat, transportation was impossible and the money was nothing."

Despite the drawbacks, Royal remembers the Hampton band as one of the most stimulating on the road. "The guys had never been anywhere. They were entirely unknown, and when we'd get somewhere, nobody would have seen them before. They had a freshness, a liveliness that was singular. The band was composed of very young people who wanted to play well. I did all the rehearsing and I rehearsed them like dogs. Because they all wanted to achieve something, they worked hard. It was one of the best bands I ever heard."

Nevertheless, by the end of 1942 some of the men were beginning to complain about the money. Jacquet and Royal left the band. "Hamp worked hell out of us," says Jacquet, "and we got ten to eleven dollars for one-nighters. When we got back to California, from not eating right and everything, I was smaller than when I left, and I'm small anyway. All he had to do was offer me some decent money."

Even without some of its original members, the band drew so well that in New York, Buckner remembers, "they started bringing us downtown in 1943. Our first downtown date was the Loew's State at Broadway and 45th Street.

Stiff upper-lipped guards have all they can do to hold back frantic fans storming the stage during a Hampton concert at London's Empress Hall in 1956. Seats were overturned and girls fainted. Hamp survived the ordeal well but the management of the Royal Albert Hall cancelled the concert his band was supposed to play there the next night.

Then we played the Strand; we did a New Year's show there at 5 a.m. The theater was packed, people three deep along the walls. Hamp was playing *Flying Home.* Some gal—she looked like Paulette Goddard—in a full-length mink coat, came up on the stage. She threw the coat into the audience and did everything that Hamp did—pounded on the tom-toms, threw drumsticks in the air, then she wanted to dance with him. But he got scared and started calling, 'Gladys!' "

Hamp's enthusiasm affects audiences, sidemen and himself. In Holland in 1956 police forcibly removed him from the stage of Amsterdam's august Concertgebouw because of the tumult he had created. One of his drummers once got carried away during a solo and began running around the Apollo stage hitting everything in sight with his sticks while Hamp hollered for Gladys. Another sideman repeatedly jumped off a barge into the Potomac River during a concert. Hamp himself "never gets offstage if he hears applause," says Jacquet. "When we were playing theaters and our part of the show was over, the movie screen would be coming forward, and Hamp was *still out there playing!*"

"Panic, uproar and pandemonium," wrote Leonard Feather in 1945, "are feeble words to describe the typical response to the Hampton version of *Flying Home.*"

Hamp's orchestra had hit its stride by 1943. It was making more money than most black bands and had singers like Joe Williams, later a smash with Count Basie, and Dinah Washington, who joined Hamp at eighteen and in three years with his band built a reputation as an outstanding blues singer.

Music began moving toward bop around 1944, and Hamp moved with it. In 1945 he appeared in Carnegie Hall as an Esquire "New Stars" leader, with Dizzy Gillespie as guest artist. He began adding to his lineup bop enthusiasts like Kenny Dorham, Fats Navarro, Art Farmer and a bass player, Charlie Mingus, later a luminary of modern jazz.

The bop arrangements sometimes conflicted with the strong, heavy beat Hamp has always emphasized. "We were playing rock before rock 'n' roll came out, around 1945-6-7," he says. "There was rockin' rhythm and rollin' rhythm. I always kept that back beat goin' in my band." And that, to the bop men, was exactly the trouble. A back beat is a strong 4/4 rhythm with heavy accents on the second and fourth beats. The rhythm gathers and controls the music. Bop arrangements, light and frothy, need a fragmented, unobtrusive beat.

On one occasion, during a broadcast from a theater, Hamp's insistence on a back beat on the drums while the band was playing a bop arrangement of Charlie's *Mingus*

37

Fingers incensed Mingus, who finally went for drummer Harold ("The Fox") Walker. "Mingus picked up the Fox," Buckner remembers, "and carried him to the back of the stage where there was an opening about six feet down. Hamp's eyes were like saucers. He kept saying, 'Don't-don't-don't drop him down there!'"

Quincy Jones, who joined the band as an eighteen-year-old trumpeter and arranger in 1951, remembers the band's bop phase. "That band was an amalgamation of the best of the young and the old. I'd look at the trumpet parts and see names like Joe Newman and Cat Anderson and think, 'I have to perform a miracle.' In those days we were the epitome of hipness, walking funny and everything. Lionel would do all those things. He was curious, interested in everything new."

One new instrument that caught Hampton's fancy and appeared for a while in his band was the Fender bass, later the foundation of all rock groups. It is an electric bass guitar whose rich, deep line underscores most rock music, adding depth to the melody and emphasis to the beat.

"A guy used to hang around with an electric ukulele," recalls Hamp. "We'd run him out of the sessions. I told him I wouldn't be able to hear it through the band. But I used him at a dance at the Shrine Auditorium in Los Angeles. Everyone said, 'Man, what's that sound coming through?' I was going on tour so I had the bass man play it. We had enough orders to put that guy in business."

Like Noah, for forty days . . .

Hamp and the band went on their first European tour in 1953, after Gladys and agent Joe Glaser talked Hamp (who hates flying) into going by air. Says Hamp: "I was gassed by the crazy reception we received everywhere." In Paris the fans staged mass demonstrations at the Olympia. They even swarmed onto the stage and danced with the men in the band. Said Hamp, "After the first night I had to fire two of the cats. I later explained to my wife, 'Gladys, they played The End—but they just couldn't dance.'"

Two years later Hamp visited Israel for the first time. A deeply religious man, Hamp carries with him everywhere a case containing the Bible and Mary Baker Eddy's Christian Science textbook, *Science and Health.* "When I play, my inspiration comes from God," he says. "My grandmother taught me to love the Bible; I count that for why I'm so hipped to Israel." Israel was hipped, too; the band went there for ten days and stayed on for forty days and forty nights.

Hamp became a fan of the late Chief Rabbi Isaac Halevi Herzog and his "beautiful Irish brogue." Deciding he'd like to say a Hebrew prayer before his concert near Tel Aviv, Hamp wrote it out phonetically. "We were playing outside in a big tent; and we were on the radio. The transmitter was seven or eight miles away. I had put the prayer on my vibes, but a breeze blew it away. I closed my eyes and said it from memory. The people said they'd never heard it said so beautifully.

"They clapped and cheered and carried on so much," continues Hamp, possibly getting carried away by his story, "they blew out the transmitter. There was a generator for the lights in the tent, and they blew that out, too."

Hampton's benefit concerts have raised thousands of dollars for the Magen David Adom, Israel's Red Cross, of which he has been made an honorary member. A visit to David's tomb inspired his *King David Suite,* a four-part, eighteen-minute work, which had its première in 1957 in New York under the direction of Dimitri Mitropoulos.

Hamp's memories stretch around the globe: jamming with Thailand's royal saxophonist, jazz-loving King Bhumibol Adulyadej; playing in Nigeria with fourteen Nigerian drummers ("*Fourteen!* It was outta sight!"); augmenting his band in Japan with Japanese musicians ("those boys can read fly specks off wallpaper"); writing the *21 Ghana Salute* to celebrate that country's independence from Britain; playing a concert in England to raise money for opponents of South Africa's apartheid policy.

When the late Joseph Cardinal Ritter was still Archbishop Ritter, Hamp worked with him to integrate parochial schools in Indiana. He has met Pope Paul VI and five American Presidents. He has been interested in politics since the first Administration of Franklin D. Roosevelt. "He was the man then. I used to be a WPA Democrat. Everybody was getting their checks from the WPA. I was playing a dance hall in Los Angeles for three or four dollars a night—they were WPA dances." He has played at inaugurals for Truman, Eisenhower, Kennedy, Johnson and Nixon, has campaigned for New York's Governor Nelson Rockefeller and Mayor John Lindsay, and has raised money for former Representative Adam Clayton Powell.

The walls of Hamp's two-room office on Manhattan's West 46th Street are covered with testimonials to his ecumenical approach to life: Thai art, souvenir keys, citations, record jackets and a large color photograph of The Hamp himself, jumping ecstatically on his tom-toms. From this headquarters, he and his staff manage the Swing & Tempo music publishing company, the Glad-Hamp Records company, his Las Vegas and Los Angeles real estate, his $13 million New York housing project and the Hampton band.

Hamp gave up his big band in 1965, saying "the more men, the more headaches," but is enjoying music more than ever with his present band of two saxes, two brass and four rhythm, which is constantly on the road swinging old and new Hampton favorites. "I'm playing things I'd forgotten I could play."

Still living at a headlong pace, Hamp burns up the calories from his enormous food intake and keeps his 5 ft. 8 in. frame in trim by hustling from one-nighter to jazz festival to concert hall to benefit appearance and taking on odd jobs in-between. In 1970 he accepted the title of Adjunct Professor of jazz at Dillard and Xavier Universities in New Orleans and promised to do something about preserving the history of jazz.

He has no plans for ever slowing down. "I like the pace," he said recently. "I like the people." — AMY LEE

In January 1971, at the Century Plaza Hotel in Los Angeles, Hampton, exuberant as ever at 60 or so, tossed his sticks and raised a tumult. Behind him are organist Johnny Spruill, Ronald Connors' trumpet and the hands of Billy Mackel, a left-handed guitarist and a Hampton sideman since 1944.

The Men Who Made the Music:
Les Brown

Lester Raymond Brown from Pennsylvania was seventeen years old and looked even younger when this picture was taken in 1929. That was during the two years he spent at the Ithaca Conservatory of Music in Ithaca, New York, along with a lot of much older students. Some of them were his brothers in Phi Mu Alpha, a national professional fraternity for musicians. Here Brown and five other nattily-clad Phi Mus line up aboard a Model T Ford, vintage c. 1917.

Raymond Brown and Thomas Dorsey were hardworking, musically gifted, single-minded men determined that their sons would have better lives than their own. They lived in northern Pennsylvania, in what natives call "the lower coal fields," where Dorsey was a miner and Brown was a baker. They first met in Pottsville when each was parading there with his hometown band, Dorsey playing trumpet and Brown playing trombone. Later, Brown played occasionally in a community band led by Dorsey in Shenandoah.

When Brown's first son, Lester Raymond, was born on March 14, 1912, Dorsey's two sons were already musicians. Tommy, then six, was getting the hang of the saxophone. Jimmy, all of eight, was playing cornet in his father's Shenandoah band. Under the firm guidance of the senior Tom Dorsey, who kept them in the house by hiding their shoes until they got their lessons right, the Dorsey boys learned rapidly. By the time Les Brown was blowing his first few notes on a soprano saxophone, the Dorsey brothers had learned almost everything their father could teach them. Within the next thirty-odd years, the volatile, violent, vibrant Dorseys made a lot of good music and earned the applause of the crowd and the informed esteem of their peers. By 1957 they were both dead. Les Brown was then —and still is—serenely enjoying the rewards of a quieter and ongoing career.

Adjectives like "easygoing" and "relaxed" have clung to Les Brown like paper clips to a magnet as he has seemingly sauntered to success by playing relaxed and charming swing. He has combined high musical and personal standards with a genial approach to life, though he, like the Dorsey boys, began his musical training under a demanding instructor. Ray Brown used to lock his son into the family bakeshop to make sure he practiced.

"Oh, boy, he was tough!" says Les. "Each day, 'Get in the bakeshop and practice!' And if he didn't hear anything for about three minutes, he'd pound on the wall."

"Teaching him was the simplest thing in the world," says Ray Brown. "When he was small he coaxed me for an instrument. So I gave him a small soprano sax. He'd come toward me and ask, 'How do you do this, Dad?' Reading music came easy for him. Everything came easy. Once, when I was arranging a quartet for saxophones, he was looking over my shoulder and said, 'I can do that, Dad.'

From Ithaca, Brown moved on to a couple of years at the New York Military Academy where he was elected leader of the cadet band. In a bunting-draped hall, the band plays for a dance with Brown, just to the left of the bass drum, playing clarinet. It was a band of diverse destinies. The trumpeter behind Brown became a dance band leader in Detroit. The drummer is a vice president of American Airlines and the saxophone player at Brown's right is a doctor.

And he did." After Les, along came his younger brothers Warren and Clyde ("Stumpy") Brown. Ray taught them both the trombone, and both of them later played amicably as sidemen in their more famous brother's band—unlike the fighting Dorseys. How did the Brown brothers get along so well? "Les was the first and started real young," says their father. "It's just the way things went."

"I'm lazy and I took the easy way," says Les. The easy way meant playing the saxophone and the piano at seven, and at ten playing his first dance date in a group called the Four Brown Brothers, made up of his father and three of his uncles. For this dressy occasion Les "borrowed a tuxedo from a guy next door who was nearly a midget."

Les grew to five feet seven inches eventually but remained boyish-looking, a fact which has never detracted from his charm on the bandstand. After a year of high school, he switched to the distinguished Ithaca Conservatory of Music in Ithaca, New York. Here he got a couple of years of training in theory, harmony and composition, plus special work in reeds and woodwinds. His teacher was Pat Conway, who was a contemporary of John Philip Sousa and no less demanding a bandmaster. A hardheaded Irishman with a rich vocabulary of profanity, Conway took a shine to Les and got him a scholarship at New York Military Academy, a well-established prep school at Cornwall-on-Hudson, where he played in the band and completed the academic requirements for college.

Les switched from his first choice, the University of Pennsylvania, to Duke University on very practical grounds. The Depression was hurting his father's bakery business, and at Duke they had a student dance band called the Blue Devils, the nickname of all Duke athletic teams. "The Blue Devils would give a free concert every night in exchange for free meals," Les recalls. "I figured if I switched to Duke at least I wouldn't starve to death."

Les joined the band as tenor saxophonist and arranger.

During his first two years at Duke, this meant mostly playing and arranging in the styles the boys learned from listening to the records of the Casa Loma and Isham Jones bands, then among the hottest outfits on the campus circuit. The Devils usually held the edge over another Duke band, the Collegians, led by Johnny Long, which copied the sweeter styles of Guy Lombardo and Jan Garber.

Les took over the band in his junior year. Under his leadership it switched to the style of the newly emerged Benny Goodman band. The switch, Les says, was easy: "I led the band with a clarinet, too." The restyled Blue Devils played not only for campus events but also for ballroom dates on weekends and vacations. They traveled in an ancient, hearse-like Cadillac, which pulled a trailer containing the instruments, the music stands and some of the sidemen.

After Les graduated in 1936, he kept the band together and signed a Decca recording contract. That fall the band went professional full time. They hit the small towns of Ohio, Pennsylvania and New York in a series of one-nighters and made a few records. They created no great stir. Most of the sidemen had not yet graduated. Now they had to choose between staying with an only marginally successful band and returning to college. By late 1937 so many of them had drifted back to school that the Blue Devils broke up. Only drummer Don Kramer, Brown's present road manager, ever played with him again.

See Harry James. Harry is pretending to bat. See Les Brown. Les is making like a catcher with a second baseman's glove. See Butch Stone. Butch is calling a strike on Harry, just like an umpire. Where is the press agent who set up this picture? He is standing in back of the photographer.

Les "rehearses" the band for a 1941 gag shot at the Log Cabin, a ballroom-farm complex in Armonk, New York. At left is Betty Bonney who sang the band's big hit that year — *Joltin' Joe DiMaggio*. Behind her is Ralph Young, male vocalist; beside her is Les's brother Warren. Next to him is

Abe Most who has helped to re-create the music of Brown and many others for the SWING ERA series. The others, from the left, are Eddie Bailey, Bob Thorne, Nat Polen, Johnnie Knepper, Eddie Scherr, Bob Fischell, Billy Rowland, Steve Madrick, Don Jacoby, Sy Zentner and Wolfie Tannenbaum.

Les moved on to New York, where he worked as a free-lance arranger for big name bandleaders like Isham Jones, Larry Clinton and his former neighbor, Jimmy Dorsey. Brown also played occasional local gigs. While temporarily leading a local band in Budd Lake, New Jersey, in 1938, he rediscovered and married Claire de Wolfe, a blue-eyed blonde he had met two years earlier when the Blue Devils played Budd Lake.

Heavy drinkers unwelcome

It turned out to be a good time to get married. RCA Victor had become interested in Brown and offered to book him into New York's Hotel Edison if he could organize a band. Backed by his father, who mortgaged the family bakery, Les got a group together in a few days. He opened at the Edison in October 1938. From the first, Les showed a knack for recruiting first-rate, dependable sidemen. "We prefer temperate musicians to teetotalers," he once said, "but heavy drinkers are unwelcome." Sidemen seemed to like Brown's firm but friendly leadership. "I try to hire gentlemen and treat them like gentlemen," says Les. Some of the gentlemen have reciprocated by sticking with Brown for decades. For the pleasures of playing with Les, some have been known to turn down offers from other bands of more than twice the salaries Brown was paying them.

Brown's 1938 group was a powerful, twelve-piece unit with a strong, steady beat. The music was clean and rendered with great precision, but somehow the outfit seemed standoffish and minus warmth. The leader was out in front blowing a slick and mellow clarinet but concentrating on the music rather than the customers. Nobody ever swooned when Les Brown came out to start the show. But as far as the sidemen were concerned he was a fine all-around leader, good at arranging and rehearsing, and his bands have always responded by giving him what he wanted— balance, imagination, consistency and, above all, tone. "Tone," he says, "is the prime requisite. By tone I mean that big, warm, round tone that, I honestly believe, gives our band a sound unlike any other."

It took a while for that first band to warm up its tone. Les himself referred to it as the "malted milk band" because nobody in it drank anything much stronger and, as he also said, "they only smoked Chesterfields" (the product of a radio-show sponsor). But as he and the band gained experience and confidence over the next couple of years, they began to spike their malted milk music with a little more zip. Brown played less ensemble and began to feature some of his excellent soloists more. The band's ballads, played in more romantic tempos than used by Goodman or Shaw, enchanted the college generation. Everybody liked Brown's pretty young singer, Doris Day, who had fled Bob Crosby's band at seventeen to escape the unwelcome attentions of one of the band members. She spent a happy year

With Les standing modestly in the background, Doris Day takes the spotlight for a vocal. She served two stints with the band before launching a movie career and helped to make *Sentimental Journey* one of the band's biggest hits.

or so among Brown's gentlemen before leaving to marry Al Jordan, one of Jimmy Dorsey's trombonists.

"Brightness of style and rightness of taste," wrote Barry Ulanov in *Metronome* in 1941, "are the most immediately striking characteristics of the Les Brown band." In 1940 the magazine had called Brown's band "99% pure." In August 1941 it gave him the other 1%. That month the band was packing them in at the Log Cabin, a combined farm and ballroom in Armonk, New York. Les and a couple of sidemen were pondering the notion of doing a song about some current celebrity. Somebody suggested Joe DiMaggio, whose fifty-six-game hitting streak for the Yankees was then hot news. Brown, with characteristic modesty, thought DiMaggio might object to having his name used by a dance band, but as it turned out neither the Yankee Clipper nor anyone else objected to *Joltin' Joe DiMaggio*.

Arranged (appropriately) by Ben Homer and belted out by teen-age vocalist Betty Bonney. Brown's recording drew a million orders. Wartime shellac shortages restricted production to 500,000, but even this limited sale helped to put the band among the top ten in the popularity polls. Though it appeared on no notable radio shows, the band got a lot of air time, and nobody laughed when a radio announcer in 1942 started calling it "the band of renown."

Renown arrived for good in 1943. Doris Day, her marriage ended, came back to the band that year and sang the vocal on *Sentimental Journey*, a new tune by Les, Bud Green and Ben Homer. There have been few better combinations for a hit than this blend of the Day voice—low, quivering, husky, but wholesome—and the Brown band with its lilting, resonant saxophones evoking a bittersweet nostalgia. *Journey* started on what appears to be a perpetual trip; it drew more than two million orders, which again were only partly filled because of the shellac shortage, and has remained a Brown-Day trademark. Like *White Christmas*, it came along at a time when a million uprooted Americans were longing for familiar scenes.

Gone with the draft

While World War II helped make *Sentimental Journey* popular, the draft gave Brown, as of course it did other bandleaders, plenty of problems. Brown was overage for the draft, but he lost plenty of sidemen. "Always the best guys seemed to go," he says. "It was like in baseball—the majors seemed to have been hit the hardest." But the demand for music increased, and Brown had all the work he could handle. In addition to the usual one-nighters, he made something like seventy-five appearances on the popular Coca-Cola Bandstand and also appeared in a few movies. Unlike some bandleaders of the period he never lowered his musical standards; he got the best sidemen he could find and paid them up to three hundred dollars a week. From 1943 to 1945, in spite of shellac shortages, the band had its biggest record sales ever—about two million a year. Only Stan Kenton and Woody Herman were pushing him.

By 1946 Les could see that television was coming in and big bands were going out. He had a son and a daughter and, as he says, "I wanted to settle in L.A. where the weather would be nice and I could relax. I had some wartime earnings and I figured I could look around for six months." He told the sidemen he was quitting. "We got loaded and cried like babies," he recalls.

Brown relaxed for just about three months. Then he learned that the management of the Palladium in Los Angeles expected him to fulfill a contract to play there. Brown had assumed that the Palladium had heard he had gone out of business and would release him. No such thing. The Palladium wanted Brown. Les hastily assembled a band including four of his old sidemen and was back in business. He never quit again.

After the Palladium there were local gigs, and then in 1947 Bob Hope's radio agent began urging Bob to hire Doris Day. Hope listened to Doris on some of her Les Brown recordings and said, "Get that band!" (The next

Aboard a C-130 plane, Brown (*left*) conducts an exhausted chorus in Christmas carols to relieve the monotony of a flight from Longbinh, South Vietnam, to Bangkok. His

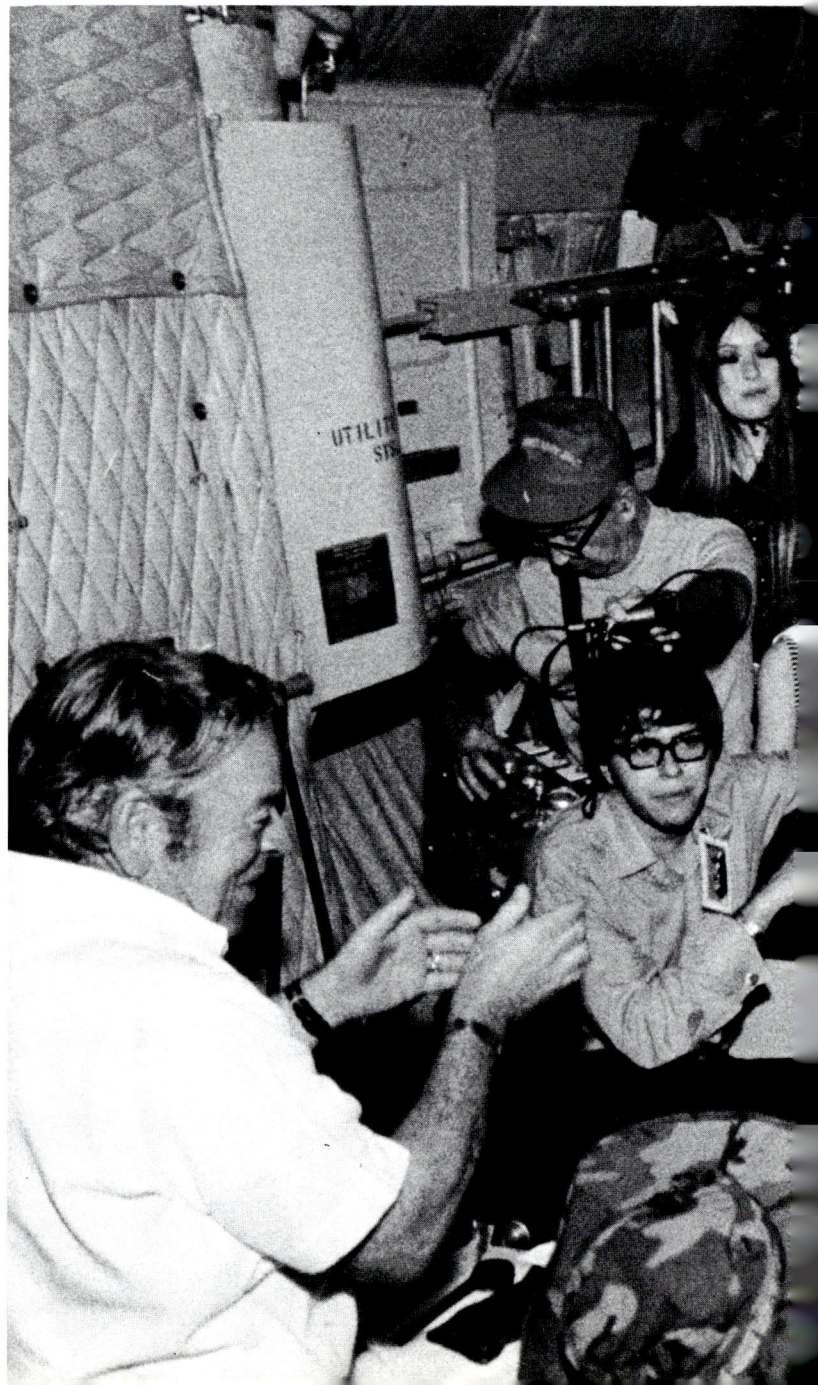

year he hired Doris, too.) The band appeared on Hope's first television show and has provided music for these occasions ever since.

The association with Hope has provided the band with various kinds of excitement, especially on its annual visits to U.S. servicemen overseas. The band arrived at one entertainment site in Korea before the Marines got there. "We had to wait for them to clear out the mines," says Les.

"Frankly, I'm a little sick of coming to the same area for the last seven years," said Brown in the middle of his 1970 Viet Nam Christmas tour with Hope, "but this is where we are needed, so this is where we come." Some of his sidemen wondered how many more tours they could stand. "I'm 58," said Butch Stone, "and I feel my age—sitting down."

Brown felt satisfied that he was keeping up with his audience. "We try to play the kind of music the average G.I. likes," he said. "Naturally, we don't play for the officers, or we'd still be playing *Sentimental Journey*."

In addition to bolstering morale abroad, the Brown band has also lent its renown to the TV performances of Frank Sinatra and Andy Williams and has anchored the Dean Martin Show since 1965. Les and the boys have achieved what strikes him as just about the perfect balance—"working two or three days a week, and for the rest, golf, swimming and bridge." He still plays the kind of music he likes best. "We prefer sound to noise," he once said. "We prefer the beat over 'effects' . . . and we like the melody if it's good." He is unruffled by the fact that his band never shared the incandescent popularity of a Glenn Miller or an Artie Shaw. "We just had a steady pull," he says comfortably. "But then, we're still here." —BRUCE HENDERSON

carolers are among 75 entertainers who helped Bob Hope put on a show which drew a standing ovation from 22,000 GIs crammed into Longbinh Bowl. The 15-day 1970 trip was the seventh Vietnam tour for Brown and the band. Les, who was then 58 and had been entertaining troops overseas ever since the Korean War, took it in stride, wearily.

By 1940 some Swing Era citizens were becoming aware of a trio with a light, bouncy, amusing and sometimes cheerfully soulful sound. It swung but never pounded. The leader's piano and the guitar skipped like water bugs along the solid stream laid down by the string bass. The leader, tall, slim and black with small eyes set at an impish angle in his handsome head, could include a whole nightclub audience in a sort of conspiracy of fun with one broad, gleaming grin. He sang with a breathy intimacy; his warm, relaxed voice had just a slight, hoarse catch somewhere in it. Anybody who ever heard that voice sing *Sweet Lorraine* or *Straighten Up and Fly Right* or *It's Only a Paper Moon* remembered it for years.

Reviewers said the voice was "purring, luscious, lulling, sugar-cured and pussywillow textured," hovering between "a weird whisper and a hoarse halloo." TIME magazine compared it to prune whip, a pull of taffy and a tranquilizing caress and said it was "three parts fog to one part frog." The voice produced every syllable of a song with effortless accuracy; the lyrics curled out of that wide mouth as unhurriedly as smoke rings. Nat ("King") Cole, who owned the voice, disparaged its quality. He often recalled the nightclub patron who told him, "I'm a doctor, boy, and with a throat like yours you should be home in bed." But Nat admitted that he had something. "Ninety percent of the popular stars today," he once said, "including myself, have no voice but they have soul. The important thing in our type of singing is . . . emotion. You can't buy it, you can't learn it. You have it or you haven't." For "soul" you could substitute "jazz." Cole was always a jazzman and never stopped sneaking a little jazz into his concerts and albums along with the sweeter stuff that earned him a fortune.

Nathaniel Adams Coles never intended to be a singer. He was born on March 17, 1919, in Montgomery, Alabama. His father, Edward James Coles, was a former grocer who had become an ordained Baptist minister. When Nathaniel was

Nat "King" Cole stands tall on a piano stool, the better to lead the band at the Sands Hotel in Las Vegas. That year, 1962, he had been in show business for a quarter century and his take for a night's work had risen from $5 to $25,000.

The Men Who Made the Music:
Nat 'King' Cole

Johnny Miller had replaced Wesley Prince on bass in the King Cole Trio when this picture, boosting a movie called *Breakfast in Hollywood*, was taken in 1945. The trio, with Oscar Moore on guitar and Cole playing the piano from a sidesaddle stance, regularly won the *Down Beat* popularity poll for small groups—every year from 1944 through 1947.

Cole had been divorced from his first wife for two years when, in 1948, he married singer Marie Antoinette (later known as Maria) Ellington (no kin to Duke), the widow of an Army Air Force pilot. The wedding was Harlem's biggest since 1923. Nearly 3,000 people, 600 of them invited, squeezed into the Abyssinian Baptist Church to hear the Rev. Adam Clayton Powell Jr. perform the service. Standing at the groom's right is his best man, his brother Eddie.

four, the Rev. Coles moved the family to Chicago and became pastor of the True Life Church on Chicago's South Side. Music surrounded Nat, his older brothers Isaac, Frederick and Edward, and their sister Evelyn. Their mother played the organ and oversaw the choir in their father's church. Like Fats Waller and Earl Hines, who came from similar backgrounds, Nat learned piano early; at twelve, he was playing the organ in church.

"We had a nice house with a lot of nice things in it," Nat once recalled. "Mama enjoyed good cooking and good music." He also remembered that he had never been made to feel inferior because he was black. He was made to feel, very strongly, that his father wanted him and his brothers to be ministers. All but Isaac became musicians. Nat never considered any other career, except maybe baseball. He was good enough to get several tentative offers from minor-league clubs, and once said, at the peak of his success, "I'd give it all up if only I could be a good baseball player."

But at fifteen, music looked like a more possible career to Nat. He had his own band then, a fourteen-piece outfit made up of high-school classmates and called the Rogues of Rhythm. They played for Saturday-night dances all over Chicago. Henry Fort played bass in that band and remem-

bered: "We couldn't play Sunday nights because Rev. Coles made us go to church." They got one dollar and fifty cents per man a night, when the gate was good enough. Sometimes they had to take out their pay in leftover refreshments.

With consummate effrontery, Nat led his schoolboy band into Chicago's Savoy Ballroom for "battles of jazz" with the powerhouse orchestra of Earl Hines, Nat's lifelong idol. Hines hints that his musicians took it easy in these contests. "We all loved Nat," Hines says. "He mimicked everything I did. He even got his musicians to buy the same olive-green jackets that my men wore." The Rogues of Rhythm copied his band's arrangements, Hines recalls, and replaced him at the Savoy when Hines was on the road. Hines used to enjoy adding a couple of new arrangements to his group's "book" just before returning to Chicago to spring on the Rogues during their next contest. Some accounts indicate that enough of Nat's South Side friends would pack the Savoy on occasion to outshout the Hines partisans.

At about this time Nat's brother Eddie returned from studying the tuba in Germany, the land of that instrument's birth and then still a Mecca for serious tuba students, and from a short stint with Noble Sissle's orchestra. Eddie joined Nat's band, gave it a bit of professional polish, and got it a six-month engagement at the Panama Cafe where Nat made eighteen dollars a week. A group called Eddie Cole's Solid Swingers, made up of the Coles brothers and four of their sidemen, cut four now very rare sides in July 1936 for the Decca "Sepia Series." The band was doing so well that Eddie was furious when Nat fell in love with Nadine Robinson, a chorus girl in the long-running Negro revue, *Shuffle Along*, and decided to accompany the show to the West Coast. The brothers came to blows and didn't speak to each other for a year after that, but off Nat went and in May 1937 he married Nadine.

Disaster followed immediately. *Shuffle Along* got the biggest audience of its tour in Long Beach, California, but folded there when one of the company vanished with the payroll. Married, broke and stranded, Nat organized a band with seven of the show's sidemen. It flopped. For the next six months or so, Nat pounded pianos in "every beer joint from San Diego to Bakersfield," as he later said, seldom making more than five dollars a night, while Nadine stayed with an aunt. Nat's marriage and his finances suffered, but he refused to go back to Chicago. "I didn't want my dad to see me busted."

Bob Lewis, who owned the Swanee Inn nightclub in Hollywood, heard Nat play one night and offered him a job —for a quartet. Nat got bassist Wesley Prince from the Lionel Hampton band at the Paradise Club in Los Angeles where Nat had often jammed. Hamp was about to join Benny Goodman and was breaking up the band. He also suggested to Nat a guitarist named Oscar Moore.

The drummer Nat hired failed to show up on opening night. The other three went on anyway. Nobody then or later missed the drums, but people did notice that the Swanee Club had a fine new trio with an extraordinary beat. Prince's bass gave it great solidity. Moore's guitar gave it great variety. Born in Austin, Texas, Moore had grown up in Phoenix, Arizona. His playing had that blue but hard-swinging sound like Charlie Christian's that seems to have originated in the Southwest. It had a springy lightness that propelled the trio, embroidered the melodies and sprang off into solo passages of joyous originality.

A song for a three-dollar customer

Nat Cole, as he called himself now, provided a firm, imaginative and highly rhythmic piano. He had something of the dazzlingly inventive, angular, polyrhythmic style he admired in Hines, and his playing would eventually influence men like Oscar Peterson and Ray Charles. At the Swanee, though, he generally subordinated his music to the trio's overall sound, which, for all its relaxed and spontaneous quality, was a carefully rehearsed product.

Singing was an involuntary addition to the sound of the King Cole Trio. (Wesley Prince thought of this name, though Cole never contradicted stories that a convivial customer had first called him "King" and presented him with a cardboard crown. "It sounds good," he once said, "so I just let it ride.") One soft autumn evening at the Swanee Inn, the trio was running through its repertory of jazz standards. A tipsy patron began insisting that Cole sing *Sweet Lorraine*. Cole protested that the trio did not sing, but Bob Lewis asked Cole to give it a try—the man was a regular who sometimes spent three whole dollars in a single evening.

Cole was a devoted family man. Here he dances with his wife's niece Carol, whom the Coles adopted, at her 1961 debut in Beverly Hills. "Cookie," as Cole always called her, has since become an actress, a wife and the mother of two.

Daughter Natalie was at college when Maria Cole Devore, who remarried after Nat died, was photographed recently with three of the Cole children—adopted son Kelly and the twins, Casey and Timolin. Cole was a baseball fan and named one of the twins for Casey Stengel. Songwriter Johnny Burke suggested a name from Irish mythology for the other.

49

Sweet Lorraine, Oscar Moore recalls, was, luckily, "one of the three or four songs that he knew then." It had been the theme song of the great jazz clarinetist Jimmie Noone when Cole was a boy in Chicago. "Just found joy," Cole sang obligingly, "I'm as happy as a baby boy, with another brand-new choo-choo toy . . ."

Cole politely returned the customer's fifteen-cent tip, as well he might; he was headed toward millions. He kept on singing and brought Moore and Prince into the vocal act, too, with a series of novelty numbers they sang in unison. The trio progressed from the Swanee Inn to bigger and better night spots, made a few records for Decca, including his first recorded version of *Sweet Lorraine*, and started to attract a little national attention. Their growing success reflected Cole's meticulous attention to details like rehearsals, dress, lighting and placement of microphones. "Make it look good," he once told jazz critic Ralph Gleason, "and it will sound twice as good." He usually looked and sounded very good indeed. Critics reported that even in normally noisy nightclub rooms, Cole's arrival on the bandstand reduced the customers to "respectful, enthralled silence."

The trio moved east, first to the Panther Room in Chicago's Hotel Sherman and then to Kelly's Stable, one of the famous string of jazz spots that once adorned New York's 52nd Street. Cole made more records, including such early popular numbers as *Babs*, *Scotchin' with the Soda* and his best blues, *That Ain't Right*. Perhaps the catchiest tune he recorded during this period was *Hit That Jive, Jack*, which introduced many of his white fans to the now-familiar "soul slap" handshake:

> "Hit that jive, Jack (*SLAP*)
> Put it in your pocket till I get back,
> Goin' down town to see a man
> And I ain't got time to shake your hand."

Soon after World War II brought the draft to the U.S., Wesley Prince left the trio to work in a defense plant. Physical disabilities like flat feet kept Cole, Moore and their new bassist, Johnny Miller, out of the service. Miller ably replaced Prince. Jazz critic Barry Ulanov reported that he "drives all the time," giving the trio as strong a beat as a drummer might have and that "you don't realize how fine Johnny is until you hear the Coles in a room."

The reluctant manager

The early Decca records sold fairly well, but Cole was still making only forty-five dollars a week, and his sidemen thirty-five, at places like Kelly's and Nick's. Then they got a triplet of breaks—a manager, a good tune and a new recording company. Honduran-born Carlos Gastel remembered: "He wanted me to manage him; he was playing in a cocktail lounge in Hollywood—skinny, big wide lapels, very good on the piano, nice singing sound to his trio . . . but manage him? I had Stan Kenton and Sonny Dunham and we were all starving."

Nevertheless Gastel took on Cole, reluctantly. He got a quick dividend after Cole signed a recording contract with Capitol, a brand-new company founded by movie producer Buddy De Silva, songwriter and singer Johnny Mercer, and Glenn Wallichs, proprietor of a Hollywood record store.

After being attacked on the stage by white racists during a show in Birmingham, Alabama, a shaken Cole, flanked by police, gets an ovation from the white crowd. "Man, I love show business," he said later, "but I don't want to die for it."

Wallichs offered Cole a contract if he would bring in the trio and also do some solo singing. Cole, less impressed than Wallichs with his own voice, hesitantly agreed. One of the first things Cole recorded for Capitol was *Straighten Up and Fly Right*, an original tune based on a sermon Cole remembered involving a buzzard who gives a monkey an aerial lift. Cole collected no royalties—he had sold all rights to the tune for fifty dollars in 1938 when he needed rent money—but *Straighten Up* put the trio on half the jukeboxes and most of the disc-jockey shows across the nation. "One night we closed at the 331 Club in Los Angeles at about $400 a week," Cole said later. "The next day we were making $1,000 at the Orpheum."

Cole followed *Straighten Up* almost immediately with another hit, *Gee, Baby, Ain't I Good to You*. Capitol promoted him and its other artists with fervor and clever publicity. His popularity zoomed. "Such a large dose of the Cole trio at one gulp has us gloriously giddy," said *Metronome* over one of the trio's first Capitol albums. Hit followed hit. He scored with the jazzy *Frim Fram Sauce* in 1945, the year *Metronome* called the trio the "Act of the Year." In 1946 his successes ranged from the imperative beat of *Route 66* to the sweet ballad *For Sentimental Reasons* to that melting marshmallow *Christmas Song*, which he recorded on a torrid August day. Cole added strings to the trio for that number. Its success marked the beginning of the decline of the trio. While *Metronome* was hailing him as "Influence of the Year"

An active Democrat, Cole was a White House guest several times during the Kennedy and the Johnson administrations. Playing host, Cole welcomes John F. Kennedy to the Beverly Hills cotillion where his daughter Carol made her debut.

for 1946 and noting the numbers of good trios that had emerged in the wake of his success, Cole was beginning to lean away from the jazz sound that had made the trio famous and toward more commercial music.

His music was paying off handsomely. Oscar Moore, who only four years before had been making thirty-five dollars a week, cleared $57,000 in 1947 in salary and royalties. At this point the trio suddenly disintegrated. Cole was being billed almost to the exclusion of Moore and Miller, and manager Carlos Gastel is said to have felt that the two sidemen were overpaid at $750 a week. Moore and Miller quit and both sued Cole, although Moore now insists that the breakup caused no hard feelings. Cole soon reconstituted the trio, with Irving Ashby on guitar and Joe Comfort on bass, and made it a quartet in 1949 by adding bongo drummer Jack Constanza. All were excellent musicians if not as brilliant as Cole's original sidemen.

Through 1948, a tough year for many big bands, Cole rode high. The group became the first Negro jazz combo to have its own sponsored radio show, and a Brooklyn-born yoga enthusiast named Eden Ahbez provided Cole with his all-time biggest hit. The bearded, long-haired Ahbez invaded Cole's dressing room and tried vainly to interest him in a tune called *I'm a Real Gone Yogi*. He also left with Cole's valet another of his efforts, *Nature Boy*. Cole selected almost all of his own material and had an uncanny sense of what people would like. He had some success in a local club

with the sugary Ahbez ditty about the "enchanted boy" who learned that love comes to those who love, so he recorded it, again using strings. The record jumped to the top of the best-seller list in ten days, and within a month had sold more than 500,000 copies. It briefly made Ahbez, who never wrote another hit, a national figure.

That year, also, Cole remarried. He and Nadine had been divorced in 1946. His new wife was Maria Ellington, no relation of the Duke's although she had sung with his band briefly. They were married by the Rev. Adam Clayton Powell Jr. in Powell's Abyssinian Baptist Church, and the reception is said to have been the second most elaborate and expensive in Harlem history. The six hundred guests consumed seventy-five pounds of coleslaw, eighteen turkeys, twenty hams, eighteen rib roasts of beef, and one hundred and ninety-seven bottles of champagne and whisky.

Nat and Maria bought a $65,000 ivy-covered brick mansion in all-white Hancock Park, one of the handsomest residential areas in Los Angeles. Signs reading "Get Out" and "Nigger Heaven" appeared on the lawn. Somebody fired a shot through a window. The retired colonel who had sold the house and the real-estate broker who had arranged the sale were threatened.

"I would like to meet all my neighbors," Cole said in a calm public statement, "and explain the situation to them. My bride and I like this house. We can afford it, and we'd like to make it our home." The neighbors sent a lawyer to tell

Cole that they did not want any "undesirable people coming into this neighborhood."

"Neither do I," said Cole. "If I see anybody undesirable coming in here, I'll be the first to complain." Eventually the neighbors simmered down and took to pointing out proudly to visitors the home of their resident celebrity. Years later, when Cole lay dying, the man the neighbors had sent around with the message about undesirable people came repeatedly to offer to do anything he could for Maria.

Until now, Cole had gracefully sidled around racial difficulties, but in the fermenting '50s the issue had become too hot and Cole too prominent to avoid confrontations. He began to sue, usually successfully, hotels that refused him lodging. Being unable to hold a grudge, he often returned to those same hotels, but the encounters increased his tensions. He was working hard and smoking heavily, sometimes having three cigarettes going at once during a recording session. An ulcer attack floored him in 1953, the year he won the *Down Beat* poll as most popular male singer. He collapsed offstage at a Carnegie Hall concert, came back out front to explain that he couldn't finish the show and went to a hospital to have half of his stomach removed. He lost seventeen pounds and remained gaunt the rest of his life.

'Aye Guy,' recording artist

The hits marched on, mostly slow ballads like *Lush Life, Mona Lisa, Unforgettable, Too Young* and the slightly more upbeat *Walking My Baby Back Home.* Cole was now using a band to back his voice on most recordings, but he still loved to play jazz. He played with the trio or the quartet in nightclubs, jammed after hours and played solid piano behind such dazzling soloists as Coleman Hawkins and Roy Eldridge in Norman Granz's Jazz at the Philharmonic concerts. (On such occasions, since he was under contract to Capitol, he used aliases like "Aye Guy.")

Along with his many hits he also made a few clinkers like *Goodnight, Little Leaguer* ("May that umpire up in heaven keep you safe tonight") and *The Little Boy That Santa Claus Forgot* ("I'm so sorry for that laddie; he hasn't got a daddy"). But he also made some marvelous offbeat records for children; *Kee-mo, Ky-mo* is perhaps unique in its blend of jazz feeling and fairy-tale atmosphere.

Cole adored his own five children and was himself a devoted son who tried vainly for twenty years to get the Rev. Coles to hear him in action. After Nat's mother died in 1955, the old man mellowed enough to attend one of his son's shows in Chicago. "I wanted to please him more than anyone I ever sang for," said Cole later. So he sang, among other things, *Faith Can Move Mountains.* "He smiled and I breathed easier. I even got up real courage and introduced him. And he took a bow."

Cole took one of his most celebrated bows in 1956 when he brought Birmingham its first big integrated stage show. Alabama racial relations were stormy then, and audiences were still segregated, but all went well at the first show, for four thousand whites, in the Municipal Auditorium, until six white men bounded up onstage and attacked Cole. Police dragged them away. The audience hollered for Nat. Bruised and shaken, he returned to the microphone and got a five-minute ovation. White editorial writers, North and South, applauded his moderate behavior, but black militants assailed him in the Negro press for "kneeling before the throne of Jim Crow" by playing to segregated audiences. Some Harlem bar owners removed his records from their jukeboxes.

Nat kept his cool. Like Duke Ellington, he felt he was helping racial understanding through his music. "I'm not a crusader," he said, but later, while under attack by militants for not leading demonstrations in the South, he raised $50,000 for civil-rights organizations. He spoke out when he thought it would help. When neither NBC nor the advertising agencies could find a national sponsor for his popular half-hour TV show, which ran for sixty-five weeks in 1956-57, he said flatly that he had been dropped because he was black and denounced TV's timidity about hiring and portraying blacks. Yet he could sympathize with the Southern TV station operator who said, "I like Nat Cole, but they told me if he came back on, they would bomb my house and my station."

Cole could almost have afforded to sponsor his own TV show. Just about everything he sang turned into gold. He toured abroad and delighted foreign fans with records in his phonetically learned and oddly accented French, Spanish, German and Japanese. In the U.S., his records sold by the million and his price for a personal appearance went to $25,000 a week. His seven film roles included a creditable portrayal of W. C. Handy in *St. Louis Blues* and a stylish cameo role in *Cat Ballou,* released after his death.

Cole shrugged off as "arthritis" the back pains that began troubling him in 1963 and refused to see a doctor. By December 1964 he was so sick that he agreed to be examined. The doctors found lung cancer, removed one lung and gave him cobalt radiation treatments. It was too late; Cole died on February 15, 1965.

Long obituaries in papers all over the country recounted the statistics of his success. He had sold fifty million dollars worth of records for Capitol, which at one time had twenty-nine of his albums in print with that handsome African mask of a face smiling from nearly every one. He had made seven "gold records"—discs whose sales were more than a million dollars apiece. He had achieved an income of almost a million dollars a year and seemed to have almost as many friends as dollars.

His friends remembered him as a rare and beautiful man. "Nat wasn't up there leading the march," said Sammy Davis Jr., "but he was there when you needed him."

His widow, Maria Cole Devore, now remarried, thought back recently to that bad day in Birmingham and Nat's dismay over the scorn of the militants. "He was so crushed at the reaction," she said. "But Nat did what he felt was right. He could have made excuses for the devil. He just thought everybody in the world had something to give."

—DAVID S. THOMSON

Splendidly nonchalant, squint-eyed with the sheer pleasure of performing—that was Nat Cole as his fans remember him best. Here he sings in *Sights and Sounds,* the second of two stage revues he organized. The show played a hundred cities and grossed a million dollars but failed to satisfy his long-held ambition to bring a production to Broadway. Two days after this picture was taken, *Sights and Sounds* closed. Cole went to the hospital; two months later he was dead.

The Music in This Volume

The war was over. So was the recording ban, under which the musicians' union, led by Petrillo (see page 18), had forbidden its members to make records. Sidemen left the services and began taking their old places on the bandstands. And the big bands got ready to resume their good old ways.

But there were casualties. Many musicians, having survived the rigors of war, were unwilling now to suffer the rigors of one-night stands on the road. One of swing's great figures, Glenn Miller, did not return at all—his plane was lost only a few months before V-E Day. Some bands had gone sadly downhill. And the vocalists, upstart offspring of the big bands, had entrenched themselves so firmly in the public favor during the recording ban (which did not apply to them) that they could not be dislodged now. The old crowds, the old enthusiasm for swing were no longer there.

The trouble was much deeper than anyone had realized until the last few weeks of 1946. Then, with catastrophic suddenness, the biggest bands in swing gave up—Tommy Dorsey, Les Brown,

Woody Herman, Benny Goodman, half a dozen others. Many came back later with new bands and some, in fact, are still playing today. But the Swing Era, as an era, was nearing its end.

You wouldn't suspect this in listening to the re-creations in this album. The music of the period had both size and subtlety, the musicians were both vigorous and inventive. Stan Kenton, prophet of a new jazz, was recording some of his most brilliant work at this time. Tommy Dorsey gave a golden sheen to a set of nostalgic old standards. Woody Herman's Thundering Herd, which was voted the best band of the period, stands as one of the best of the whole era. Gene Krupa, Lionel Hampton and Les Brown showed a relish for the fresh, astringent harmonies of progressive jazz.

Adding to its sound, its techniques and its sources, swing would live on into the next two decades. Looking back today, these postwar years have a sunset glow. But it was a very brave display, for the music is still hot, brilliant and bold. Though the era had ended, swing had not.

SIDE ONE

Band 1 CHICAGO
Tommy Dorsey version

Of all the hymns to a hometown that songwriters have written, the least reverent is certainly *Chicago*. Nobody ever takes his hat off when the band breaks into "CHI-*CA*-GO, CHI-*CA*-GO, that tod-dl-in' town (tod-dl-in' town)" or grows teary at thoughts of "State Street, that great street . . ." What the song is more likely to bring on is a creaky finger-snapping or a gimpy Charleston.

The man who wrote this paean wasn't a Chicagoan by birth or for very long. Fred Fisher showed up in the Windy City around the turn of the century with a sailor's walk (he said he acquired it in the German Imperial Navy, which he joined at the age of thirteen), a scar on his cheek (a souvenir, he explained, of a hitch in the Foreign Legion) and a strong animal smell in his clothes (from the cattle boat, he said, that brought him over). Nobody, happily, has ever tried to confirm or disprove these legends or Fisher's story that he learned to play the piano in a single lesson from a pianist in a South Side saloon.

Nobody, of course, could ever question Fisher's genius as a popular songwriter. His compositions include *Come Josephine in My Flying Machine, Peg O' My Heart, There's a Little Spark of Love Still Burning, When It's Moonlight on the Alamo, Ireland Must Be Heaven (For My Mother Came from There).* And, switching musical hats, he wrote the lyrics for *Dardanella.* By the time success had overtaken him, Fisher had left Chicago

for New York. *Chicago* still brings in $700 or $800 a week in royalties, which soar at political convention time when the local bands are always breaking patriotically into the tune.

Tommy Dorsey's version passes the melody happily around from the lyric trombone, to the graceful muted trumpet, to the flowing clarinet to the snappy vocalists, to the tenor sax (which manages to get an eight-bar solo out of one note) and on to band and brass. In the original version, the chorus was sung by Sy Oliver, the arranger. In this SWING ERA re-creation, Sy's part is taken by his old companion in the Lunceford band, Trummy Young (who also sings Sy's arrangement of *Margie* in the 1938-39 album of THE SWING ERA). Since the Dorsey version was recorded, the words of *Chicago* have been changed to appease the civic pride of some oversensitive Chicagoans. In the original lyrics Chicago was a place that Billy Sunday couldn't shut down. This has become "The folks who visit it all wanna settle down." And that line about the man who danced with his own wife becomes, in the bowdlerized version, "Bring all your friends, your kids and your wife." But Trummy and this re-creation are faithful to the impious original, and here CHI-*CA*-GO is still the town where Billy Sunday flopped and husbands do strange things.

Band 2 SEPTEMBER SONG
Harry James version

As a young man Walter Huston did some vaudeville hoofing and singing. But by 1938, when he was hired for a leading role in a Broadway musical called *Knickerbocker Holiday*, he had become a distinguished dramatic actor, noted for his portrayal of the old husband in O'Neill's *Desire Under the Elms*.

Having engaged Huston, Kurt Weill and Maxwell Anderson, the show's authors, realized they had no notion of how he sang. They wired him: "What is the range of your voice?" The actor wired back cheerfully: "I have no range." But he added that he was appearing with Bing Crosby on the radio that night and would venture a few bars. Listening, Weill and Anderson discovered that their new star wasn't exactly a Caruso and wrote the score accordingly. "I flew out to see Huston," recalls Josh Logan, who directed the show. "I read him the script and sang him the score. But he wanted a love song to sing to the girl. I promised him he could have one, and when I flew back I told Anderson and Weill about a new song. They said it would be impossible—but wrote *September Song* that day."

September Song was tailored to Huston's rough, untutored tones. And when he sang it onstage as the peg-legged Pieter Stuyvesant wooing a girl half his age, the audience always wanted to hear it again. Huston grew so weary of singing the same words over and over that he persuaded Anderson to write a set of lyrics just for his encores. "No one ever wrote these lyrics down," says Logan, "but I remember them and they go: 'But it's a long long while from May to December/And you've won or lost when you reach September/And I'm no cavalier and my compliments are lame/And my gambling days are done for I've won my game/And the wine dwindles down to a precious brew, September, November/And these few vintage years, I'd spend with you/The vintage years, I'd spend with you.' "

The show did not last long on Broadway, and Huston's love song was almost forgotten. Eight years later Huston revived it for a comedy called *Apple of His Eye* in which he again played the part of a middle-aged man wooing a young girl. About this time, Bing Crosby recorded it and so did Harry James. The James version opens with a hesitant figure that continues as the trombones play the melody. All is very restrained until, abruptly, the phrasing gets gutsy, and the trumpet (James in the original) bursts out, not with the pleading of a middle-aged man, but with the demands of a hot-blooded lover. These recordings called new attention to the song but, surprisingly, the one that became the biggest jukebox favorite was Walter Huston's own version.

By now, crooners, operatic tenors, balladeers and lady vocalists have all recorded *September Song*. Lotte Lenya, Kurt Weill's widow, remarks that Jimmy Durante has sung it "just beautifully." But nobody has ever matched the belligerent pathos of Huston's rendition, which stands, along with Rex Harrison's *I've Grown Accustomed to Her Face*, as a tribute to the art of a singer who has hardly any singing voice.

Huston's son John, the film director, remembers that his father "loved every minute of singing *September Song*. I thought he was extremely moving despite the fact that he almost talked the song. He was, in fact, very musical and was an accomplished performer on the harmonica." (Huston senior played a memorable harmonica number in his son's film, *The Treasure of Sierra Madre*.) "I remember one song my father wrote and used to sing in vaudeville," John goes on. "It was called 'I Haven't Got the Do-Re-Mi,' and one verse went: 'I would go to Turkey on the fastest ship that sails/I'd have the ladies comb my hair and manicure my nails/But I haven't got the do-re-mi/No, I haven't got the do-re-mi.' "

Band 3   HIGH ON A WINDY TRUMPET
Les Brown version

Some of the strident sounds and tight tempos of postwar jazz push through in *High on a Windy Trumpet*. The quick beat is set by piano and rhythm and, after the muted trumpets play the melody, the saxes fall into a succession of weird harmonies. The trombone adopts the raw and brilliant tone coming into fashion at the time while even the velvety tenor goes briefly modern. But the solo of the title is in the Berigan trumpet tradition, playing the high ranges with lovely tone and thoughtful phrasing.

High on a Windy Trumpet was written by Bob Higgins, who composed *Lover's Leap* heard on Side 6 of this album. He first named it *High on a Windy Saxophone* as a comment, he explains, on the breathy style of sax players like Ben Webster and Zoot Sims. But Brown, Higgins says, didn't get the joke and changed the name. Brown says he changed it because Jimmy Zito added such a great trumpet solo to it.

Higgins played trumpet in Brown's band for eight years and gave it up to enter business after having gone back to college. He graduated first in the class of '52 at the University of Southern California's School of Commerce, and wound up as vice-president in charge of international operations of Denny's Inc., which operates some 1,000 restaurants and doughnut shops in several countries. Today, sitting in his office in La Mirada, California, the ex-horn player feels a little wistful that he never fulfilled his dream of composing for Duke Ellington. Being part of THE SWING ERA series helps to make up for that. "I groove over the idea," he says, "that twenty-five years later someone is making a reissue of those tunes. To think they survived makes me feel good."

Band 4   MIDNIGHT SUN
Lionel Hampton version

As Hamp remembers the birth of *Midnight Sun*, "I was doing a picture called *A Song Is Born*, a kind of takeoff on *A Star Is Born*, and there were a lot of jazzmen working on it—Louis and Benny and Tommy and Charlie Barnet. When we got tired of waiting around the studio, I used to jam on the piano, and the stagehands and electricians all wanted me to play *How High the Moon*. I'd play it day after day, and one day I got tired of playing it and went into this little riff. Sonny Burke was musical director of the film and heard it and said: 'Hey, what's that?' So I did it again. A couple of days later Sonny told me he had something for me and he'd bring it over. He played it for me and I said: 'Hey, that's what I was playing a couple of days ago.' We played it and everybody loved it."

Sonny Burke remembers it a little differently. When he first heard it, Hamp was warming up at the vibes—not the piano. "The way Hamp is, he's not happy unless he's performing, even when he's only rehearsing. I stopped him after a dozen notes and said, 'That sounds like a great tune'; and he didn't even remember what he'd played so I played it back to him." Why the title? "It just sounded right for the tune."

The melody of *Midnight Sun* has a long line, and the vibraphone spins it out with strong and bell-like tones—no tinkling or quavering. Saxes and trumpets play with feeling and the vibes come back for a last eight bars, running a delicate embroidery on the melody. Hampton made his mark with loud, fast-flying crowd senders. But he also loves ballads and soft songs, and he proves his devotion soulfully in *Midnight Sun*.

Band 5   INTERMISSION RIFF
Stan Kenton version

Coming up to intermissions at the Palladium in Los Angeles, the Kenton band would announce the break with a bouncy riff they had used as background for their performance of *Body and Soul*. As riffs have a way of doing, it began to get longer and bigger and eventually it was in the Kenton book as *Intermission Riff*.

With the first statement of the riff, the piano sets a perky, disjointed beat. The trombones take it up, barking the theme, and the trumpets, in typical Kenton style, come on with

55

a countertheme. A solo tenor sax keeps noodling over the brass and cymbals, and a strong-voiced ensemble leads into a breezy trombone chorus. The sections push the piece until the riffing quiets down and gives up in a whirl of tom-toms.

Compared to the driving head arrangements that Count Basie and Woody Herman used to make out of their riffs, Kenton's is a relatively restrained and cerebral work. But though Stan used to proclaim that he didn't "think jazz was meant to continue as dance music," *Intermission Riff* shows that he can play for people's feet as well as for their heads.

SIDE TWO

Band 1 TENDERLY
Randy Brooks version

The Salvation Army can boast of having some swinging trumpeters among its musical alumni. Harry James, as an eleven-year-old horn player in his father's circus band, used to help out with hymns on the sidewalks of Beaumont, Texas. Randy Brooks played for the Army in Sanford, Maine, when he was only six. At ten, a big-lunged prodigy, he could rip through the showiest passages of *Carnival of Venice*; at eleven, he played with Rudy Vallee on a radio program. A couple of years later he abandoned the classics for jazz. At twenty-four he was a sideman for Hal Kemp and later for Claude Thornhill and Les Brown. In 1945 he formed his own band, building it around his trumpet. He played with a fantastic skill that sometimes lapsed into pure show-off and with a tone that sometimes went schmaltzy but never lost its plangent beauty.

George Barden, who arranged *Tenderly*, remembers that Brooks in 1946 had fallen madly in love with Ina Ray Hutton, the singer and bandleader. She was with him one night when Walter Gross, the composer, first played *Tenderly* for Brooks. "They decided," says Barden, "that it was 'our song,' and Randy told me to make an arrangement right away so he could play it for her that night. In an hour and a half I had the chorus written out and the band went through it once, and when Ina Ray walked in that night it made a big impression on her."

The piece is all Randy's, the trumpet loudly announcing itself, dropping into the melody, rhapsodizing in the improvisations, taking a full-toned chorus with chromatic sighs. Then it goes up and up and stays there, never losing its roundness or control. Eddy Shomer, a Brooks sideman, still shakes his head and says: "That guy could play in the high range—double high C—all night and with the greatest of ease."

The men who played with Brooks admired him enormously as a trumpeter. "He did things on the horn in those days," says Paul Lajoie, his bass player, "that I still don't hear anybody doing today. He was almost unlimited as to flexibility and range." But some musicians couldn't work with Randy as a leader. "He wasn't the nicest man in the world," remarks Lajoie. "He was a supreme egotist, and he just didn't get along with his men. I must have seen eighty or ninety, possibly even a hundred guys go through the band during the time I was with him."

Brooks married Ina Ray, broke up his band to tour with her, separated from her and, after suffering a series of strokes, he died tragically in a fire. Phil Napoleon, New Orleans trumpeter who led the famous Memphis Five half a century ago, knew Brooks well and remembers him "as a kid who had an unhappy complex about not being wanted by the rest of the boys. He had a great talent. I used to boast about him as a kid who could put some of the big names like James and a few others in his vest pocket. It's a pity he died so young. Old Gabriel has taken a lot of these kids too soon. What a trumpet section he has up there!"

Band 2 CHLOE
Tommy Dorsey version

Whoever it is that has been lookin' through the dismal swamp and callin' and cryin' for Chloe started his mournful search back in 1927. By that time, Charles N. Daniels, *Chloe's*

creator, was already a widely known popular composer—though not under that name. Back in the 1890s, when Daniels started his career by writing a march for John Philip Sousa, it was the fashion for composers to adopt European names, preferably French ones. So Daniels called himself Neil Moret. As Moret, he wrote the first movie theme song, *Mickey*, done for the picture of that name starring Mabel Normand, the loveliest of the Mack Sennett bathing girls; and *Moonlight and Roses*, which every ukulele-playing swain of the 1920s plunked out interminably for his sweetheart. Later Moret wrote *She's Funny That Way* and *Sweet and Lovely*.

For *Chloe*, his collaborator was Gus Kahn, the veteran lyricist. Mrs. Kahn recalls that "when they were finished with the song, they were all enthused. Then Gus turned to me in dismay and said, 'I wrote this song and never once mentioned Chloe in the chorus.' They were concerned but finally decided to leave it because it was so right it couldn't be better and, besides, the name was all through the verse. Chloe, by the way, was just a name Gus made up."

In Dorsey's version, which was filled by arranger Bill Finegan with tricks and variations and unexpected chords, the tom-toms thud along with the horns until the brass gives out with the first call of "Chloe." The baritone sax calls back, the tom-toms keep on and all at once, the trombones are singing "Through the black of night, I got to go where you are." The trumpets move on through the smoke and flame, and the saxes come in at "Ain't no chains can bind you." The second chorus has a series of short attractive solos—piano, trumpet, tenor sax and finally the clarinet, which pipes its way into the ending.

By now, people have lost track of the countless *Chloes* that have been recorded. Dorsey's is one of the most attractive, but the biggest seller of all was the one Spike Jones made in 1942 full of fire engine bells and corny gags. It was an outrageous parody, but when Neil Moret heard it just the year before he died he wasn't at all upset. In fact, says his daughter, he was rather pleased. "If anything is good enough to parody," he remarked, "it has to be a success." And Gus Kahn's spirited widow remembers that "one day after Gus had died, Jerome Kern called me up and he was beside himself. 'Grace,' he said, 'you've got to do something. There's a record by Spike Jones, and he's just massacring Gus's lovely *Chloe*.' 'All right, Jerry,' I replied, 'I'll get the record.' I did and—well, I just loved it. I was too ashamed ever to mention it to Jerry again."

Band 3 DREAM
Pied Pipers version

The Pied Pipers were originally a vocal octet who sang with Tommy Dorsey in the late '30s. But Dorsey couldn't afford eight singers and the Pipers left in 1938. Pretty soon, Tommy pulled some of them back and put together a more economical group, a quartet with Jo Stafford as lead singer. Eventually, the quartet left Dorsey and then Stafford left them. June Hutton was the lead singer in 1944 when the Pied Pipers made their most famous number, *Dream*.

For *Dream*, the Pied Pipers backed themselves up with a twenty-piece band which, led by Paul Weston, played a rich accompaniment to the low-keyed harmonizing of the voices. Helping enormously was a pure-toned tenor sax solo, played originally by Eddie Miller. "I'm still remembered for that little solo," says Eddie, who now plays at Pete Fountain's in New

Orleans, "and I still get a big hand when I play it."

The song itself was written by Johnny Mercer and arranged by Paul Weston. "We needed a closing theme for the new Chesterfield radio program that Johnny was getting together," Weston recalls, "and one morning before the show began I went by his house. He told me he had this song. That is, he had the tune and lyrics, but he didn't know what chords he wanted. So we sat down for a bit and found him the chords. Chesterfield thought the song was absolutely great, especially that part with the words 'Dream, while the smoke rings rise in the air.' It was like another commercial."

Bands 4 and 5 CONCERTO TO END ALL CONCERTOS Parts I and II
Stan Kenton version

"Most of all," Stan Kenton once remarked, "a musician needs affection. He has to be told when he plays well, applauded at the right time; he has to be shown that he is respected, and must get enough bows to satisfy his ego." Kenton had this in mind when he wrote *Concerto To End All Concertos*. "It was

created as a showcase for everybody in the band," he explains, "a chance for the boys to take solos. We put a comical title on it, but when Capitol recorded it, the title stuck."

The first solo is taken on the piano—it was Stan in the original giving his plaintive theme a romantic treatment. The next soloist, coming on after the brass, is the tenor sax (originally Vido Musso), playing in the dark, emotional style of the great Coleman Hawkins. The trumpet screams its solo, and an agile alto sax speeds through a chorus over the double bass until, with striding chords, Part I of the *Concerto* ends.

The soloists are all but forsaken in Part II as the sections take over. First the trombones, broad and solemn, repeat the opening theme. The saxes and a dancing beat change the mood. The trumpets change it again with an ethereal passage over the bass. The trombones march down the scale while the trumpets go up and, with tom-toms and big chords, the end-all *Concerto* ends. Kenton crammed a great deal into this one package—nineteenth century symphonic sound, progressive jazz, a little Wagner, a bit of Ellington. It may sometimes seem a little too much, but there's always something happening.

SIDE THREE

Band 1 I'VE GOT MY LOVE TO KEEP ME WARM
Les Brown version

"We'd finished at the Palladium in L.A. one night back in 1946," recalls Les Brown, "and had to go straight to a recording date. Well, the session went fine, and we had twenty minutes of studio time left over. We got out *I've Got My Love To Keep Me Warm,* which we'd taken along as an extra, and breezed through it. But the record company didn't release it—the song had been around for a few years ever since Irving Berlin wrote it for Dick Powell in some movie [it was *On the Avenue* with Powell, Madeleine Carroll, Alice Faye and the Ritz Brothers]. Anyway, the record company forgot all about it. A couple of years later I was playing on Bob Hope's radio show, and we did *I've Got My Love* right after Bob's opening monologue. The record company sales manager happened to be listening and I got a wire from him: 'Record that number right away.' I wired back: 'Look in your files.' There it was, of course. So they put it out and it took right off. Even Irving Berlin wrote me a nice letter about it."

The number has the friendly conversational air that Brown got into so much of his work. The saxes bounce into the introduction. The trumpets build to little bursts of sound. The piano falls into a solo full of clean chords and runs, and a muted trumpet plays the melody with feeling. For a late starter, *I've Got My Love* did phenomenally well. Of all Brown's recordings, it was second in sales only to the one in which Doris Day sang her unforgettable *Sentimental Journey* (re-created in the 1944-45 album of THE SWING ERA).

Band 2 I SHOULD CARE
Tommy Dorsey version

In 1944 Paul Weston was living in a Los Angeles apartment house distinguished for its Hibernian-Iberian name, the Casa Argyle, and for its musicianly tenants. Among them were the composer Axel Stordahl and the lyricist Sammy Cahn. One day Weston hummed a couple of notes to Stordahl and Cahn and asked them: "Do you think this could be made into a song?" It was a slim start, but Stordahl sat down with Weston and in a couple of days they had a melody. Cahn quickly wrote words for it, and Tommy Dorsey quickly added it to his band's book.

Bill Finegan, arranging *I Should Care,* put in something for everybody Dorsey had in the band at the time, which meant writing for five saxes, eight brasses and four rhythm, a tuba, nine strings, a girl singer and a vocal group. The number starts

lushly, with trembling strings and soft brass. The solo singer comes in ruefully. The vocal group joins in smoothly, the ensemble is smooth and the trombone (originally Tommy's) was never smoother.

At this time Paul Weston was thirty-two and established in the music business—which he got into, quite literally, by accident. A Phi Beta Kappa out of Dartmouth, he was preparing to conquer Wall Street in 1934 when he was hurt in an automobile smashup. During a six-month convalescence, he resumed the musical tinkering he had done at college and, when he was all better, kept right on as arranger and composer. *I Should Care* was his first standard, his first composition to become part of the popular repertory. Although he probably has since had his name—as composer, arranger or leader—on more records (an estimated eighty million) than anybody else, he still speaks warmly of this first success. "It's been very good to me," he says. "Every couple of years someone else records it." He likes the 1945 Dorsey version, but his favorite is the one Jo Stafford made in 1961, by which time she was Mrs. Weston.

Band 3 HAMP'S WALKIN' BOOGIE
Lionel Hampton version

Lionel Hampton has always been partial to boogie-woogie tunes and has recorded seven of them: *Hamp's Boogie Woogie, Three Quarter Boogie, Two Finger Boogie, Tempo's Boogie* (Tempo was the name of his black Scottie), *Beulah's Boogie, Beulah's Sister Boogie* and *Hamp's Walkin' Boogie.* This last isn't very different from *Hamp's Boogie Woogie* (re-created in the 1944-45 album of THE SWING ERA), but it does have a fillip. "I used to walk around when I played it," Hamp explains, "so we added a little walking-around music."

The piano walks the boogie first, at a steady pace. The vibraphone takes over and the boogie begins to swing. The ensemble roars in, and the boogie strides under a high trumpet. The piano does a repeated-note figure, the vibes echo it, the boogie clumps along—and suddenly disappears. The vibes run down the scale, the band runs up, everybody swings, and the boogie never comes back—and nobody seems to care.

Band 4 AFTERNOON IN AUGUST
Billy Butterfield version

"Any musician with any ambition always wanted to have his own band," says trumpeter Billy Butterfield. "With me, the war interfered. But as soon as I got out of the Army, I started my band. It was great having it." Like so many other musicians who realized their ambition, Butterfield discovered he was more successful as a player than a leader. When he did what came naturally and concentrated on his trumpet, his band would sound first-rate—as it did in *Afternoon in August*. The first trumpet solo, played over an interesting combination of major and minor chords, is big and straightforward. In the second chorus the trumpet jumps into the high registers, clear and clean, and ends on a gently turned phrase.

This album of THE SWING ERA re-creates the way three trumpeters of the time played numbers that are all touched by a melancholy autumnal feeling. The Randy Brooks approach in *Tenderly* on Side 2 is immensely attractive and skillful if a little self-conscious in achieving its effects. The Harry James re-creation recalls, in the tone colors of *Autumn Serenade* on Side 6, the self-assured old hand, not afraid to be sweet but careful never to get sticky. The Billy Butterfield part in *Afternoon in August* has a kind of innocence. It is played with a clarity that gives the tone an almost transparent quality and with a restrained power that suggests that, if the trumpet really let go in the recording studio, it would blow out the whole works.

Band 5 SHERWOOD'S FOREST
Bobby Sherwood version
Among the things Bobby Sherwood has done in his overcrowded career are play the banjo (at age nine) in his par-ents' vaudeville act, provide guitar backgrounds for Bing Crosby and Lily Pons, play trombone and piano in several bands, arrange and compose songs, work several years as a successful disc jockey, act brilliantly in a Broadway play and lead one of the most un-kempt swing bands ever to make the big time.

Its music wasn't sloppy, however, though it was often odd. "In *Sherwood's Forest*, I was looking for a little different sound," Bobby says in a masterly understatement. *Sherwood's Forest* sometimes sounds like a B-movie chase. Other times it sounds as though the band were putting on Stan Kenton (as in *Concerto* on Side 2). It also sounds like a serenade to Dracula, and for a while it sounds like just a plain old swing flag-waver. All in all it is played more for tromping than for dancing. But if, like its leader in his search for a career, the band never makes up its mind what it wants to be doing, it has a very good time trying a little of everything.

The title is as clear as everything else. "We had wanted to call it *Duel in the Sun*," says Sherwood, who today is settled and successful as the leader of a combo in Las Vegas, "and actually printed the labels with that name and put them on 50,000 records when we learned the title belonged to a big new movie. So we changed to *Sherwood's Forest*. We had to stick the new labels over the old, and anyone who peeled the top label off wouldn't know what he was getting." It might have been simpler all around if Sherwood had stuck with his first title. "Originally," he says, "we called the number 'Bedlam.' "

SIDE FOUR

Band 1 AT SUNDOWN
Tommy Dorsey version
The sounds of an earlier jazz era keep trying to break through on Tommy Dorsey's version of *At Sundown*, the great old standard that the old song master Walter Donaldson wrote back in the 1920s. Bill Finegan arranged it for a 1946 movie called *The Fabulous Dorseys* and gave it period sound to fit a scene where Tommy and Jimmy were playing in Paul Whiteman's band. But in rearranging it for the Dorsey record, Finegan muf-fled a lot of the 1920s and let in a little of the modern mid-'40s. "Still," says Billy May, conductor of most of these re-creations for THE SWING ERA, "the Whiteman period comes through where the phrasing is a little tight and the attack a little staccato."

At Sundown opens with a flaring ensemble but quickly gets to the familiar melody, with Dorsey in the original leading the trombones. "Tommy was playing good then," Billy May re-members. The trombones shift to a stern marching figure and work with the saxes into an odd modulation. The tenor sax plays in short, graceful phrases with trumpets scooping out a strange sound in back. The muted trumpet (originally Charlie Shavers) comes on for a superb thin-voiced solo. The saxes have a crazy sliding figure, the melody tootles in, and the sun goes down in a quiet chord.

Band 2 RACHEL'S DREAM
Benny Goodman version
Rachel Goodman was only two years old when her fond father dedicated this little improvisation to her. It was a happy dream he imagined for his first-born, and his sextet romped through it with a gay mix of sounds and solos—clarinet, piano and vibes together, the clarinet in some startling octave jumps, a self-assured piano pushed back by a swaggering bass which is upstaged by the vibes. Rachel grew up to be a musical girl, a pianist who has played Debussy and Beethoven in a couple of father-daughter concerts. She doesn't play jazz—"classical music is easier," she believes—but she writes about it. In a magazine, she once described her father's first meeting with the Beatles.

This confrontation between the young rulers of rock and the old King of Swing stopped dead in its tracks when Paul McCartney remarked to Benny, "It's the same with all those big swing bands —rather fruity arrangements."

Band 3 THE MAN WITH THE HORN
Randy Brooks version
This might have been written with Randy Brooks and his trumpet in mind, so suited is it to the sweet strength of his tone, his ecstatic breaks, his easy virtuosity. He put his mark on the piece at the start of his first chorus, the horn coming in low and quiet, leaping briefly into the high register. In the second chorus the technical display starts. The trumpet soars, doubles the time and plays full-toned improvisations. Three spectacular leaps —in high, middle and low register—brace the listener for further dazzling work. Instead, the trumpet plays a soft reminder of the melody and goes quietly off.

But *The Man with the Horn* was not composed for Brooks or even, in fact, for a trumpet. Bonnie Lake, the singer-composer, wrote it for her husband, Jack Jenney, who was an extraordinarily talented trombonist—his memorable chorus in Artie Shaw's *Stardust* is re-created in the 1940-41 album of THE SWING ERA. But Jenney died in 1945 before he had a chance to record *The Man with the Horn*. "It's been recorded as a solo for just about every instrument in the band," says Miss Lake, "even once for the oboe. But it's never been done by a trombone."

Band 4 BIJOU
Woody Herman version
The beginning of *Bijou* catches the ear right away—an exotic coupling of piano and guitar, an intricate drum rhythm be-hind the trumpets, an overwrought tenor sax. But this is simply a prologue to one of the most famous trombone performances in swing's history, played originally by Bill Harris.

The trombone announces itself bluntly. Then it sud-denly softens and moves into a complex melody over a Latin background, the raw sweetness of the tone giving the rude horn an unexpected poignance. It breaks its mood with a succession of octave jumps, but drops back into its breathy softness. When the trombone returns after the ensemble, it is no longer easy and yielding but tense, repeating a two-note cry and then an urgent three-note figure before it leaves.

Of all the many fierce and lovely and funny performances Bill Harris has given in his jazz career, *Bijou* is the best remembered, a landmark that influenced a whole generation of trombonists after him. A professorial-looking musician who seemed almost demure on the bandstand, Harris played with driving speed in fast passages, a polished vibrato in ballads and a sense of humor that can be heard in two Herman numbers re-created in the 1944-45 album of THE SWING ERA: *Apple Honey* and *Wildroot*. But for all his talent, he almost didn't make it in swing because he couldn't read music—a deficiency that put Harris in distinguished company. Dozens of great jazzmen had trouble reading notes—Bix Beiderbecke, for example, and Herschel Evans and the trumpeter Wingy Manone, who once complained: "I can read notes easily enough, but I can't separate 'em."

Inability to read lost Harris his first big chance—he lasted only a week with Gene Krupa in 1938. He sweated out his problem and improved enough to land a job with Benny Goodman who overlooked Bill's deficiencies because of his wild and exhilarating way with his horn. Harris went over to Herman in 1945 and Woody asked Ralph Burns, his pianist-arranger, to write a number for him. *Bijou* was the result. "It was something I used to diddle around with on the piano," says Burns. "Woody or maybe it was Chubby Jackson, who played the bass, heard me playing it and told me to write it down. I named it after a friend's cat. I was over at her house and told her I was looking for a title, and the cat's name seemed logical." Harris still gets requests for *Bijou* and still enjoys playing it. But he's surprised at its success. "When I first played it, I didn't have any feeling at all about it. Truthfully I didn't—it didn't seem like a hit to me."

Band 5 ARTISTRY IN RHYTHM
Stan Kenton version

The best known of Stan Kenton's compositions was played for years before it was given a name. It began, as noted in the article on Kenton in the 1944-45 album of THE SWING ERA, as the theme that introduced his band on its radio broadcasts—which always opened with an invitation to hear "the artistry in rhythm of Stanley Kenton." By the time Kenton was making records, the theme was a full-fledged number—but still nameless. A contest among radio listeners brought some pretty farfetched titles—*Hoboken Concerto, Arctic Night*—and the record company was just about to settle for *Topaz* when the boss decreed that the piece should be called something that meant Kenton. So it became *Artistry in Rhythm.*

It earns the title through the ingenious ways Kenton brings about a series of rhythmic and harmonic changes. The stately brass that starts it off is interrupted by the quickening tom-toms, and soon the band is speeding in several directions: the saxes taking the melody, the trombones snapping replies, the trumpets blowing above. The piano plays an introspective chorus, then doubles the tempo with some left-hand notes that the bass picks up. Now the trumpets have the melody, then the saxes over an emphatic beat. When the trombones take it, the rhythm switches again. Drum rolls and big chords end the number.

"The great thing about *Artistry in Rhythm*," says Shelly Manne, who was drummer in Kenton's band, "was that it was so identifiable—there was no doubt whose orchestra it was. The dramatic impact was a very important part of it. And one of the most important things about the band was its drama—something that's almost never considered."

SIDE FIVE

Band 1 LOVER
Gene Krupa version

One of the most shocking and satisfying things about swing was the outrageous way bands would mistreat and manhandle an established tune—and come up with a brilliant work. Tommy Dorsey polished off Rimsky-Korsakov in *Song of India* (THE SWING ERA, 1936-37 album). John Kirby transformed *Anitra's Dance* (THE SWING ERA, 1938-39 album). And Gene Krupa took Richard Rodgers' *Lover*, written for Jeanette MacDonald in the movie *Love Me Tonight*, and gave it a rocketing run that left the lilting waltz breathless but still beautiful.

"What a tempo," Krupa himself once said, admiring what he had done. "It's strictly what we used to call a killer-diller. But isn't that band clean! That's Charlie Ventura on tenor and Don Fagerquist on that nice muted trumpet, and that wild trombone is Leon Cox." He hardly had to mention that that dervish on the drums in the original was Gene Krupa. Fast cymbals set the pace for the swift, muted-trumpet melody and equally swift sax countermelodies. The saxes indulge in a little looping waltzy figure before the trumpets are back. Tenor sax dashes in, followed by trumpet with alto on its heels, then band, drums, band, more drums, trombone swipes, and, never letting up, everyone races to the finish.

The speed of any piece of music is measured by its reading on a metronome, a device that ticks away the tempo. A very fast piece—for example, Benny Goodman's *Rachel's Dream*, re-created on Side 4 of this album—has a metronome count of 264. *Lover*, as arranged for Krupa by Eddie Finckel, comes in at a fantastic 312. But for all its flying succession of solos and ensembles, the niceties of technique and tone give *Lover* a certain ease, a kind of headlong daintiness.

Band 2 THEN I'LL BE HAPPY
Tommy Dorsey version

"A tune I always loved," said Cliff Friend, remembering back nearly fifty years, "was *Goodbye, My Lady Love* by Joe Howard—he also wrote *I Wonder Who's Kissing Her Now.* I used to play it in various ways and I guess it became the basis of *Then I'll Be Happy.* When I'd written the tune and the words, I called up Lew Brown to get his help on the lyrics. I read him what I'd done: 'If I could go where you go, If I could do what you do, If I could be where you are, Then I'd be happy.' 'Cliff,' Lew said, 'right away you've got a problem. Too many ifs. You gotta be more definite.' So I took the ifs out and made it more definite: 'I wanna do what you do, go where you go . . .' And that little difference Brown suggested was all the difference between a nothing and a big hit."

Twenty years later, Sy Oliver revived the old hit for Tommy Dorsey and gave it the kind of easy-going but driving arrangement he used to write for the Lunceford band in its heyday. In the beginning, the clarinet peeps and the trombones give a kind of caw before moving into the melody. The saxes play smoothly under the warm solo trombone, then have a give-and-take with the muted trumpet—here the sax cutoffs sound very Luncefordian. The tenor sax, soft and graceful, sings over whomping brass, the clarinet peeps in again and the bass walks the piece out.

When he composed *Then I'll Be Happy* in 1924, Cliff Friend was becoming a composer full time. He had already written *Mama Loves Papa, There's Yes, Yes in Your Eyes* and *You Tell Her, I Stutter* and went on to write *Tamiami Trail, The Merry Go Round Broke Down* and *Trade Winds,* along with several Broadway shows and Hollywood musicals.

A spry, sharp man, he was living in Las Vegas when he died in 1974 at the age of 80. He once said of *Then I'll Be Happy,* "that's still one of my favorite songs."

Band 3 BLOWIN' UP A STORM
Woody Herman version

In early jazz talk, a musician always "blew" a wind instrument, never merely played it. After a while he blew any instrument, wind or not. "You been blowin' piano a long time?" one musician would ask another. Eventually the word meant to do anything. In *A Jazz Lexicon*, Robert S. Gold quotes a sideman as remarking of a friend: "He blows a great conversation" and another as complimenting a cook with "She blows scrambled eggs from endsville." The use of the word was extended: "Blow down" meant to beat; "blow the gig" meant to not show up for an engagement; "blow up a breeze" or "blow up a storm" meant either that a band worked hard or that it created great excitement. This latter was intended to apply to this Woody Herman number when, out of a list of titles suggested by radio listeners for one of the band's improvised arrangements, he chose *Blowin' Up a Storm*.

Storm gets off comfortably with a fetching piano and rhythm chorus on a twelve-bar blues theme. The clarinet flutters over a discreet background, and the band, using the flatted fifths of progressive jazz, runs through some chromatic passages. Guitar and bass have a lovely quiet stretch, but the band comes back, trumpet screaming, and storms along until it rumbles off.

Bands 4 HAPPY-GO-LUCKY LOCAL Parts I and II
and 5 *Duke Ellington version*

Like so many composers—from Arthur Honegger, whose symphonic *Pacific 231* celebrates a famous type of locomotive, to Meade Lux Lewis, whose boogie-woogie depicts a *Honky Tonk Train* (THE SWING ERA, 1938-39)—Duke Ellington has had a long love affair with trains. He expressed it first in *Lightnin'*, written in 1932. Then came *Daybreak Express* (1934). His longest and most loving description was *Happy-Go-Lucky Local*, the last movement of the *Deep South Suite*, which he composed in 1946.

Here the Duke wasn't suggesting a train, he was duplicating it—a clanking, hooting, bouncing local, stopping at every little station along a backwoods line to nowhere. The piano, bass and deep saxes get the wheels started, alto sax and wah-wahing brass push it on. With the brass chugging and the reeds wailing, the train rocks along, a trumpet blowing hard and the piano and bass coming in to give more momentum. As Part II starts, the piece jounces along a stretch of syncopated piano and bass, picks up in a surging passage by the reeds. The brass answers and takes up the theme. The clarinet makes a smooth run, the piano pounds along, the trumpet lets off steam and the nimble bass brings the local kerplunk to a stop.

You may find in Part II a section that sounds familiar but that you don't associate with Ellington. This section was virtually lifted out of *Happy-Go-Lucky Local* and made into *Night Train*, a much-recorded hit of the 1950s. Ellington disliked some of the versions, which were made without consulting him, but he did nothing about it. "It hurts and it's offensive," he once told Stanley Dance, author of *The World of Duke Ellington*. "You threaten to sue and you postpone until it's too late and then you get real mad. You do nothing but spoil your disposition." Well, *Night Trains* come and go, but they can't spoil the happy disposition of Duke's musical rattler.

SIDE SIX

Band 1 THE GOOD EARTH
Woody Herman version

When this tune was first set down by Neal Hefti, it was called "Helen of Troy." It turned out that another band had done an instrumental using that title, so somebody suggested *The Good Earth*. It was a natural selection, according to Hefti. Pearl Buck's novel of that name was famous, and so was the movie made from it. This, however, wasn't the only reason that the band liked the title. In sidemen's slang, "good earth" meant marijuana.

The whole piece is motion and power. Bass and drums have a clout; cymbals churn; the sax tones thicken the textures. Some listeners used to feel almost overpowered by this Herman band, the first of his Thundering Herds. But in *The Good Earth* the big sound does not lapse into noise, and the band keeps a firm rein on itself. The unison saxes take the catchy theme first, and the piano tries to set up a little dialogue with them. The ensemble gets into the conversation, and the clarinet (originally Herman) rises above it, sounding a little like Artie Shaw. The volume grows and a heavy-toned tenor saxophone takes over, continuing into the ensemble passage. The sax section moves in and the band tries to end the piece, but the clarinet slips back to take a little three-note bow. "It was a matter of not cutting our endings too short," Woody says, "so I just ad-libbed a few notes."

Band 2 AUTUMN SERENADE
Harry James version

Back in 1945 Billy May, conductor of these re-creations for THE SWING ERA, was given a ballad by Harry James and told to make an arrangement for it. "I thought whoever composed it was good," Mays says. "I did a little different arrangement from most of the things Harry had then, but then the tune was a little different." Billy's arrangement surprised Harry's sidemen. They knew May as a jazz writer, and here he had suddenly turned into a tone poet.

For *Autumn Serenade* he brought in an instrument strange to swing bands, the English horn, which is neither English nor a horn but a low-voiced oboe. His arrangement starts with sweeping trumpets and trilling strings leading into the trumpet solo, played (originally by James) with a heartfelt vibrato that beautifully matches the mood of the song. In a fine solo, the tenor sax plays lightly over trombone doo-wahs, and after more trumpet and a string interlude, the English horn and valve trombone come on in unison. Muted trumpets and a too-brief alto sax follow, the English horn and trombone come back again, the serenade swells to a crescendo and dissolves in some autumnal chords.

The composer of *Autumn Serenade*, by the way, was Peter De Rose. He wrote *Wagon Wheels, Deep Purple* and *Rain*, but was for years better known as the partner and husband of May Singhi Breen, radio's "Ukulele Lady." From the early 1920s to the late '30s, the two of them touched the hearts of millions of listeners as the musically devoted "Sweethearts of the Air."

Band 3 ROUTE 66
Nat King Cole version

Geography has helped songwriters to produce such immortal numbers as *Springtime in the Rockies, Moonlight in Vermont* and *Carolina in the Morning*, but Bobby Troup got his inspiration from studying a road map. He was just out of the Marines and eager to resume a promising musical career—a song called *Daddy* that he had written as a college senior had made the Hit Parade on a Sammy Kaye record. Leaving Chicago for California, he took Route 66 all the way to Los Angeles, where he met Nat King Cole. "Nat liked a tune I'd written called *Baby, Baby All the Time*," Troup remembers, "but asked me if I had anything else. So I played him half a song I'd made up in the car driving to the Coast. He asked me to finish it and bring it back. Well, there was no piano in the motel I was staying at, so I went over to the old NBC studios on Vine Street, and I'd go from one rehearsal studio to the next, looking for one that wasn't being used—and always keeping the road map of my trip with me. I'd work until the musicians came in, and then I'd move on with my map. Cole liked the song and rushed the recording through. When he got around to doing *Baby*, it was also a hit."

Cole recorded *Route 66* first in 1946 and again, years later, in the version heard in this album. Cole was then recording almost nothing but lushly orchestrated ballads, but he had not lost his jazz feeling, as can be plainly heard in his playing and singing and in the blending of his piano with the guitar and bass. The song gave a special identity to Route 66. Troup says that every town along the way had the record in its jukeboxes; shops still sell postcards saying, "I got my kicks on Route 66." But Oscar Moore, who played guitar with Cole, remembers the time a disgusted customer came in to hear the trio and bawled them out: " 'I took Route 66 into L.A., and I want to shoot all three of you guys. It's the worst road I've ever been on.' He was right, but *Route 66* was always popular—the song, I mean, not the road." The song gained a new popularity in the mid-1960s when the Rolling Stones recorded it. With them, it's a different and more hard-driving journey than the one Cole took.

Band 4 CARNEGIE BLUES
Duke Ellington version
His first concert in Carnegie Hall in 1942 was a frustrating experience for Duke Ellington. The audience was ecstatic —"DUKE KILLS CARNEGIE CATS" was *Metronome's* headline. But the critics were very reserved about a suite Ellington had written for the occasion. *Black, Brown and Beige* ran for forty-five minutes and was the Duke's most ambitious work up to then. Disappointed, the Duke salvaged a section of the suite —a short instrumental interlude in the long vocal section called The Blues—and made a separate piece of it. He gave it the wry title of *Carnegie Blues* and the music seems to be not so much mourning the occasion as mocking it. After the saxes and piano start things off, the brass takes the blues theme with an assist

from the bass. The piano returns to bring on the tenor sax, which wails in and is met by muted comments from the trombone. Trumpets, unaccompanied, form a bridge to the wah-wahs of trombones and saxes whose complaints end the lament.

The tenor sax solo was originally taken by Al Sears, who is more or less responsible for the theme of *Carnegie Blues*. "We were fooling around in the band with the background for a number called *My Little Brown Book*," he says. "I did a little ditty on the sax, and Duke said: 'I want to buy that.' So later, I was doing bad in a poker game and I sold it to him and he worked it up. Duke knew how to place what he heard—he was the greatest compiler I ever knew."

Band 5 LOVER'S LEAP
Les Brown version
"We had a trumpet player named Bob Higgins," says Les Brown, "who was a good songwriter. But he was lazy and didn't write much. Once in a while we'd be at rehearsal and he'd say: 'Hey, I wrote something.' "

Lover's Leap was by this lazy trumpeter, who also composed *High on a Windy Trumpet*, re-created on Side 1 of this album. It was no sudden inspiration. "That song was a thing I walked the streets with," Higgins explains, "hearing snatches here and there and then sitting down to write it when it all came together."

The piano starts brightly, then keeps breaking into the chorus—which, incidentally, gets a special lilt from unexpected accents (on the four-*and* beat in every second measure). The alto plays buoyantly, and the band tries some wild tone mixtures, with a stop-time routine that recalls Glenn Miller's *In the Mood* (THE SWING ERA, 1940-41 album). The pleasant rhythm of *Lover's Leap*, the exact but relaxed ensemble work, the skillful—though not showstopping—solos, all these explain why Brown, who was slighted by some swing critics, has proved so popular and enduring. At a time when jazz was beginning to take itself very seriously, *Lover's Leap* carried on in the traditions of the Swing Era when the music held simpler excitement and pleasure for the players and the listeners. —JOSEPH KASTNER

The Musicians Who Made the Recordings in This Volume

CHICAGO
LEADER: Billy May TRUMPETS: John Audino, John Best, Uan Rasey, Shorty Sherock TROMBONES: Joe Howard, Lew McCreary, Lloyd Ulyate, Dick Nash SAXOPHONES: Skeets Herfurt, Abe Most, Justin Gordon, Don Raffell, Chuck Gentry PIANO: Ray Sherman GUITAR: Jack Marshall BASS: Rolly Bundock DRUMS: Nick Fatool SOLOS: Dick Nash (trombone), Shorty Sherock (trumpet), Abe Most (clarinet) VOCAL: Trummy Young VOCAL GROUP: Sue Allen, Peggy Clark, Ann Clark Terry, Betty Jane Baker

SEPTEMBER SONG
LEADER: Billy May TRUMPETS: John Audino, Shorty Sherock, John Best, Uan Rasey TROMBONES: Joe Howard, Dick Nash, Lloyd Ulyate, Lew McCreary SAXOPHONES: Abe Most, Chuck Gentry, Les Robinson, Justin Gordon, Don Lodice VIOLINS: Sid Sharp, Mischa Russell, Nat Kaproff, John de Voogdt, Spiro Stamos, Irving Geller, Jack Gootkin, Eddie Bergman, Ted Rosen, Paulo Alencar VIOLAS: Lou Kievman. Al Harshman, Myron Sandler CELLOS: Ray Kelley, Nino Rosso, Igor Horoshevsky PIANO: Ray Sherman GUITAR:

Jack Marshall BASS: Rolly Bundock DRUMS: Nick Fatool SOLO: Joe Graves (trumpet)

HIGH ON A WINDY TRUMPET
LEADER: Billy May TRUMPETS: John Audino, John Best, Uan Rasey, Shorty Sherock TROMBONES: Dick Nash, Joe Howard, Lloyd Ulyate, Lew McCreary SAXOPHONES: Skeets Herfurt, Abe Most, Justin Gordon, Don Raffell, Chuck Gentry PIANO: Ray Sherman GUITAR: Jack Marshall BASS: Rolly Bundock DRUMS: Nick Fatool SOLOS: Dick Nash (trombone), Pete Candoli (trumpet), Justin Gordon (tenor saxophone), Ray Sherman (piano)

MIDNIGHT SUN
LEADER: Glen Gray TRUMPETS: Pete Candoli, Conrad Gozzo, Manny Klein, Uan Rasey, Shorty Sherock TROMBONES: Milt Bernhart, Joe Howard, Tommy Pederson, George Roberts, Si Zentner SAXOPHONES: Chuck Gentry, Skeets Herfurt, Plas Johnson, Babe Russin, Willie Schwartz PIANO: Ray Sherman GUITAR: George Van Eps BASS: Mike Rubin DRUMS: Nick Fatool SOLOS: Emil Richards (vibraphone), Shorty Sherock (trumpet)

INTERMISSION RIFF
LEADER: Glen Gray TRUMPETS: Pete Candoli, Conrad Gozzo, Manny Klein, Uan Rasey, Shorty Sherock TROMBONES: Milt Bernhart, Joe Howard, Tommy Pederson, George Roberts, Si Zentner SAXOPHONES: Skeets Herfurt, Chuck Gentry, Willie Schwartz, Babe Russin, Plas Johnson PIANO: Ray Sherman GUITAR: George Van Eps BASS: Mike Rubin DRUMS: Nick Fatool SOLOS: Plas Johnson (saxophone), Milt Bernhart (trombone)

TENDERLY
LEADER: Glen Gray TRUMPETS: Conrad Gozzo, Shorty Sherock, Pete Candoli, Manny Klein TROMBONES: Si Zentner, Murray McEachern, Joe Howard, Benny Benson SAXOPHONES: Skeets Herfurt, Gus Bivona, Babe Russin, Chuck Gentry, Julie Jacob PIANO: Ray Sherman GUITAR: Jack Marshall BASS: Mike Rubin DRUMS: Nick Fatool SOLO: Shorty Sherock (trumpet)

CHLOE
LEADER: Billy May TRUMPETS: John Audino, Shorty Sherock, John Best, Bud Brisbois TROMBONES: Joe Howard, Lew McCreary,

Lloyd Ulyate SAXOPHONES: Les Robinson, Justin Gordon, Abe Most, Don Raffell, Chuck Gentry PIANO: Ray Sherman GUITAR: Jack Marshall BASS: Rolly Bundock DRUMS: Nick Fatool SOLOS: Pete Candoli (trumpet), Dick Nash (trombone), Abe Most (clarinet), Justin Gordon (tenor saxophone)

DREAM
LEADER: Billy May TRUMPETS: John Best, Shorty Sherock, Uan Rasey TROMBONES: Dick Nash, Lloyd Ulyate SAXOPHONES: Les Robinson, Abe Most, Don Lodice, Chuck Gentry VIOLINS: Sid Sharp, Mischa Russell, Nat Kaproff, John de Voogdt, Spiro Stamos, Irving Geller, Jack Gootkin, Eddie Bergman, Ted Rosen, Paulo Alencar VIOLAS: Lou Kievman, Al Harshman, Myron Sandler CELLOS: Ray Kelley, Nino Rosso, Igor Horoshevsky CELESTE: Ray Sherman GUITAR: Jack Marshall BASS: Rolly Bundock DRUMS: Nick Fatool SOLO: Justin Gordon (tenor saxophone) VOCAL GROUP: Sue Allen, William Brown, Alan Davies, Jerry Whitman.

CONCERTO TO END ALL CONCERTOS
Parts I and II
LEADER: Billy May TRUMPETS: John Audino, Shorty Sherock, John Best, Uan Rasey, Chuck Findley, Bud Brisbois TROMBONES: Joe Howard, Dick Nash, Lloyd Ulyate, Lew McCreary, Ken Shroyer SAXOPHONES: Skeets Herfurt, Abe Most, Justin Gordon, Don Raffell, Chuck Gentry PIANO: Ray Sherman GUITAR: Jack Marshall BASS: Morty Corb DRUMS: Nick Fatool SOLOS: Ray Sherman (piano), Plas Johnson (tenor saxophone), Bud Brisbois (trumpet), Morty Corb (bass), Justin Gordon (alto saxophone)

I'VE GOT MY LOVE TO KEEP ME WARM
LEADER: Billy May TRUMPETS: John Audino, Shorty Sherock, John Best, Uan Rasey, Bud Brisbois TROMBONES: Joe Howard, Dick Nash, Lew McCreary, Lloyd Ulyate SAXOPHONES: Les Robinson, Justin Gordon, Abe Most, Don Raffell, Chuck Gentry PIANO: Ray Sherman GUITAR: Jack Marshall BASS: Rolly Bundock DRUMS: Nick Fatool SOLOS: Justin Gordon (tenor saxophone), Shorty Sherock (trumpet), Ray Sherman (piano)

I SHOULD CARE
LEADER: Billy May TRUMPETS: John Audino, Shorty Sherock, John Best, Uan Rasey TROMBONES: Joe Howard, Lew McCreary, Lloyd Ulyate TUBA: John Bambridge SAXOPHONES: Les Robinson, Abe Most, Justin Gordon, Don Lodice, Chuck Gentry VIOLINS: Sid Sharp, Mischa Russell, Nat Kaproff, John de Voogdt, Spiro Stamos, Irving Geller, Jack Gootkin, Eddie Bergman, Ted Rosen, Paulo Alencar VIOLAS: Lou Kievman, Al Harshman, Myron Sandler CELLOS: Ray Kelley, Nino Rosso, Igor Horoshevsky HARP: Verlye Mills PIANO: Ray Sherman GUITAR: Jack Marshall BASS: Rolly Bundock DRUMS: Nick Fatool SOLO: Dick Nash (trombone) VOCAL: Eileen Wilson VOCAL GROUP: Sue Allen, Billie Barnum, Peggy Clark, Ann Clark Terry

HAMP'S WALKIN' BOOGIE
LEADER: Billy May TRUMPETS: John Audino, Uan Rasey, Chuck Findley, Bud Brisbois, Joe Graves TROMBONES: Joe Howard, Dick Nash, Lew McCreary, Lloyd Ulyate SAXOPHONES: Les Robinson, Abe Most, Justin Gordon, Don Lodice, Chuck Gentry PIANO: Ray Sherman GUITAR: Jack Marshall BASS: Rolly Bundock DRUMS: Nick Fatool SOLOS: Larry Bunker (vibraphone), Ray Sherman (piano), Bud Brisbois (trumpet)

AFTERNOON IN AUGUST
LEADER: Glen Gray TRUMPETS: Pete Candoli, Conrad Gozzo, Uan Rasey, Manny Klein, Shorty Sherock TROMBONES: Milt Bernhart, Joe Howard, Ed Kusby, George Roberts SAXOPHONES: Gus Bivona, Chuck Gentry, Skeets Herfurt, Julie Jacob, Babe Russin PIANO:

Ray Sherman GUITAR: Jack Marshall BASS: Mike Rubin DRUMS: Nick Fatool SOLOS: Shorty Sherock (trumpet), Gus Bivona (clarinet), Skeets Herfurt (alto saxophone)

SHERWOOD'S FOREST
LEADER: Glen Gray TRUMPETS: Pete Candoli, Conrad Gozzo, Manny Klein, Uan Rasey, Shorty Sherock TROMBONES: Milt Bernhart, Joe Howard, Tommy Pederson, George Roberts, Si Zentner SAXOPHONES: Skeets Herfurt, Willie Schwartz, Gus Bivona, Babe Russin, Plas Johnson BASSOON: Chuck Gentry PIANO: Ray Sherman GUITAR: George Van Eps BASS: Mike Rubin DRUMS: Nick Fatool

AT SUNDOWN
LEADER: Billy May TRUMPETS: John Audino, John Best, Bud Brisbois, Uan Rasey, Chuck Findley TROMBONES: Lloyd Ulyate, Dick Nash, Joe Howard, Lew McCreary SAXOPHONES: Skeets Herfurt, Abe Most, Justin Gordon, Don Raffell, Chuck Gentry PIANO: Ray Sherman GUITAR: Jack Marshall BASS: Morty Corb DRUMS: Nick Fatool SOLOS: Shorty Sherock (trumpet), Justin Gordon (tenor saxophone), Lloyd Ulyate (trombone)

RACHEL'S DREAM
LEADER: Billy May CLARINET: Abe Most PIANO: Ray Sherman GUITAR: Jack Marshall BASS: Rolly Bundock DRUMS: Nick Fatool VIBRAPHONE: Larry Bunker

THE MAN WITH THE HORN
LEADER: Billy May TRUMPETS: John Audino, Uan Rasey, Bud Brisbois, Chuck Findley TROMBONES: Joe Howard, Dick Nash, Lew McCreary, Lloyd Ulyate SAXOPHONES: Les Robinson, Abe Most, Justin Gordon, Don Lodice, Chuck Gentry PIANO: Ray Sherman GUITAR: Jack Marshall BASS: Rolly Bundock DRUMS: Nick Fatool SOLOS: Joe Graves (trumpet), Justin Gordon (tenor saxophone)

BIJOU
LEADER: Billy May TRUMPETS: Shorty Sherock, John Best, Pete Candoli, Uan Rasey, Bud Brisbois TROMBONES: Joe Howard, Dick Nash, Lloyd Ulyate, Dick Noel SAXOPHONES: Skeets Herfurt, Les Robinson, Justin Gordon, Don Raffell, Chuck Gentry PIANO: Ray Sherman GUITAR: Al Hendrickson BASS: Rolly Bundock DRUMS: Nick Fatool SOLOS: Skeets Herfurt (alto saxophone), Abe Most (clarinet), Dick Nash (trombone)

ARTISTRY IN RHYTHM
LEADER: Glen Gray TRUMPETS: Conrad Gozzo, Shorty Sherock, Joe Graves, Uan Rasey, Manny Klein TROMBONES: Ed Kusby, Joe Howard, Milt Bernhart, Lew McCreary SAXOPHONES: Abe Most, Skeets Herfurt, Justin Gentry, Chuck Gentry, Plas Johnson PIANO: Ray Sherman GUITAR: Jack Marshall BASS: Mike Rubin DRUMS: Nick Fatool SOLO: Ray Sherman (piano)

LOVER
LEADER: Billy May TRUMPETS: Shorty Sherock, John Best, Uan Rasey, John Audino, Bud Brisbois TROMBONES: Joe Howard, Lew McCreary, Lloyd Ulyate, Dick Nash SAXOPHONES: Skeets Herfurt, Les Robinson, Justin Gordon, Plas Johnson, Chuck Gentry PIANO: Ray Sherman GUITAR: Jack Marshall BASS: Rolly Bundock DRUMS: Nick Fatool SOLOS: Justin Gordon (tenor saxophone), Nick Fatool (drums), Dick Nash (trombone), Shorty Sherock (trumpet)

THEN I'LL BE HAPPY
LEADER: Billy May TRUMPETS: John Audino, John Best, Bud Brisbois, Uan Rasey, Chuck Findley TROMBONES: Lloyd Ulyate, Dick Nash, Joe Howard, Lew McCreary SAXOPHONES: Skeets Herfurt, Abe Most, Justin Gordon, Don Raffell, Chuck Gentry PIANO: Ray Sherman GUITAR: Jack Marshall BASS: Morty Corb DRUMS: Nick Fatool SOLOS:

Shorty Sherock (trumpet), Justin Gordon (tenor saxophone), Morty Corb (bass), Abe Most (clarinet), Joe Howard (trombone)

BLOWIN' UP A STORM
LEADER: Glen Gray TRUMPETS: Conrad Gozzo, Manny Klein, Joe Graves, Shorty Sherock, Uan Rasey TROMBONES: Joe Howard, Milt Bernhart, Lew McCreary, Si Zentner SAXOPHONES: Abe Most, Skeets Herfurt, Plas Johnson, Babe Russin, Chuck Gentry PIANO: Ray Sherman GUITAR: Jack Marshall BASS: Mike Rubin DRUMS: Irv Cottler SOLOS: Abe Most (clarinet), Jack Marshall (guitar), Ray Sherman (piano), Shorty Sherock (trumpet)

HAPPY-GO-LUCKY LOCAL Parts I and II
LEADER: Billy May TRUMPETS: John Audino, Uan Rasey, Joe Graves, Chuck Findley, Bud Brisbois TROMBONES: Dick Nash, Joe Howard, Lew McCreary SAXOPHONES: Les Robinson, Abe Most, Justin Gordon, Don Lodice, Chuck Gentry PIANO: Ray Sherman GUITAR: Jack Marshall BASS: Rolly Bundock DRUMS: Nick Fatool SOLOS: Ray Sherman (piano), Rolly Bundock (bass), Pete Candoli (trumpet), Justin Gordon (alto saxophone), Chuck Gentry (baritone saxophone), Bud Brisbois (high trumpet)

THE GOOD EARTH
LEADER: Billy May TRUMPETS: Shorty Sherock, John Best, Uan Rasey, Frank Beach, Bud Brisbois TROMBONES: Joe Howard, Lew McCreary, Lloyd Ulyate SAXOPHONES: Les Robinson, Willie Schwartz, Justin Gordon, Julie Jacob, Chuck Gentry PIANO: Ray Sherman GUITAR: Jack Marshall BASS: Rolly Bundock DRUMS: Nick Fatool SOLOS: Abe Most (clarinet), Justin Gordon (tenor saxophone)

AUTUMN SERENADE
LEADER: Billy May TRUMPETS: Pete Candoli, Shorty Sherock, John Best, Uan Rasey TROMBONES: Joe Howard, Lew McCreary, Lloyd Ulyate, Dick Noel SAXOPHONES: Skeets Herfurt, Abe Most, Justin Gordon, Julie Jacob, Chuck Gentry VIOLINS: Paul Shure, Jerry Vinci, Sid Sharp, Eddie Bergman, Irving Geller, John de Voogdt, Mischa Russell, Darrel Terwilliger, Spiro Stamos, Harold Dicterow VIOLAS: Sam Boghossian, Lou Kievman, Gary Nuttycombe CELLOS: Armand Kaproff, Fred Seykora, Ray Kelley PIANO: Ray Sherman GUITAR: Al Hendrickson BASS: Rolly Bundock DRUMS: Nick Fatool SOLOS: Joe Graves (trumpet), Justin Gordon (tenor saxophone), Julie Jacob (English horn), Skeets Herfurt (alto saxophone)

ROUTE 66
PIANO AND VOCAL: Nat King Cole GUITAR: John Collins BASS: Charlie Harris

CARNEGIE BLUES
LEADER: Billy May TRUMPETS: John Audino, Shorty Sherock, John Best, Bud Brisbois, Uan Rasey TROMBONES: Joe Howard, Lew McCreary, Lloyd Ulyate, Dick Nash SAXOPHONES: Les Robinson, Justin Gordon, Abe Most, Don Raffell, Chuck Gentry PIANO: Ray Sherman GUITAR: Jack Marshall BASS: Rolly Bundock DRUMS: Nick Fatool SOLOS: Ray Sherman (piano), Justin Gordon (tenor saxophone), Lew McCreary (trombone)

LOVER'S LEAP
LEADER: Billy May TRUMPETS: John Audino, Shorty Sherock, Uan Rasey, John Best TROMBONES: Joe Howard, Dick Nash, Lew McCreary, Lloyd Ulyate SAXOPHONES: Les Robinson, Justin Gordon, Abe Most, Don Raffell, Chuck Gentry PIANO: Ray Sherman GUITAR: Jack Marshall BASS: Rolly Bundock DRUMS: Nick Fatool SOLOS: Justin Gordon (alto saxophone), Bud Brisbois (trumpet), Ray Sherman (piano)

ORCHESTRA MANAGER: Abe Siegel
MIXER: Rex Updegraft

Discography

The original recordings of the selections re-created in this volume

---

CHICAGO
Composer and lyricist: Fred Fisher. Arranger: Sy Oliver. Recorded for Victor September 7, 1945
TRUMPETS: George Seaberg, Vito Mangano, Gerald Goff, Charlie Shavers TROMBONES: Tommy Dorsey, Karl De Karske, Tex Satterwhite, William Hallar SAXOPHONES: Sid Cooper, Buddy De Franco, Bruce Branson, Babe Fresk, Harry Steinfeld PIANO: John Potoker GUITAR: Sam Herman BASS: Sid Block DRUMS: Buddy Rich VOCALS: Sy Oliver and The Sentimentalists (°Peggy, °Ann, Jean and Mary Clark)

SEPTEMBER SONG
Composer: Kurt Weill. Arranger: Ray Conniff. Recorded for Columbia November 6, 1947
TRUMPETS: Harry James, Pinky Savitt, Nick Buono, Gene Komer, Ralph Osborn TROMBONES: Ziggy Elmer, Victor Hamann, Charlie Preble, Juan Tizol SAXOPHONES: Willie Smith, Ed Rosa, Corky Corcoran, Sam Sachelle, Bob Poland STRINGS: Unknown PIANO: Bruce McDonald GUITAR: Tiny Timbrell BASS: Ed Mihelich DRUMS: Bud Combine

HIGH ON A WINDY TRUMPET
Composer and arranger: Bob Higgins. Recorded for Columbia March 27, 1946
TRUMPETS: Jimmy Zito, Don Jacoby, Al Muller, Bob Higgins TROMBONES: Don Boyd, Warren Covington, Dick Gould, Stumpy Brown SAXOPHONES: Steve Madrick, Mark Douglas, Ted Nash, Eddie Scherr, Butch Stone PIANO: Jeff Clarkson GUITAR: Hy White BASS: Bob Leininger DRUMS: Dick Shanahan

MIDNIGHT SUN
Composers: Sonny Burke and Lionel Hampton. Arranger: Sonny Burke. Recorded for Decca November 10, 1947
TRUMPETS: Wendell Culley, Duke Garrette, Snooky Young, Teddy Buckner, Leo Shepard TROMBONES: James Robinson, Andrew Penn, Jimmy Wormick, Britt Woodman SAXOPHONES: Jack Kelson, Bobby Plater, Ben Kynard, Morris Lane, John Sparrow, Charlie Fowlkes PIANO: Milt Buckner GUITAR: Billy Mackel BASS: Joe Comfort, Charlie Mingus DRUMS: Earl Walker VIBRAPHONE: Lionel Hampton

INTERMISSION RIFF
Composer and arranger: Ray Wetzel. Recorded for Capitol January 14, 1946
TRUMPETS: Ray Wetzel, John Anderson, Russ Burgher, Bob Lymperis, Buddy Childers TROMBONES: Fred Zito, Milt Kabak, Ray Klein, Bart Varsalona SAXOPHONES: Al Anthony, Bob Gioga, Boots Mussulli, Vido Musso, Bob Cooper PIANO: Stan Kenton GUITAR: Bob Ahern BASS: Eddie Safranski DRUMS: Ralph Collier

°Took part in one or more of the re-creations in this volume

TENDERLY
Composer: Walter Gross. Arranger: George M. Barden Jr. Recorded for Decca July 14, 1947
TRUMPETS: Randy Brooks, Chuck Mederios, Guy Erlandsen, Al Muller TROMBONES: Dave Pitman, Marshal Hawk SAXOPHONES: Danny Barteluce, Art Lopez, Patrick Balbo, Eddy Shomer PIANO: Shorty Allen BASS: Paul Lajoie DRUMS: Sonny Mann

CHLOE
Composer: Neil Moret. Arranger: Bill Finegan. Recorded for Victor September 20, 1945
TRUMPETS: George Seaberg, Vito Mangano, Gerald Goff, Charlie Shavers TROMBONES: Tommy Dorsey, Karl De Karske, Tex Satterwhite, William Hallar SAXOPHONES: Sid Cooper, Buddy De Franco, Bruce Branson, Babe Fresk, Dave Harris PIANO: John Potoker GUITAR: Sam Herman BASS: Sid Block DRUMS: Buddy Rich

DREAM
Composer and lyricist: Johnny Mercer. Arranger: Paul Weston. Recorded for Capitol December 6, 1944
TRUMPETS: Charles Griffard, Don Anderson, Nate Kazebier TROMBONES: Al Thompson, Joe Yukl SAXOPHONES: Doc Rando, Eddie Miller, Hap Lawson, Matty Matlock, Lennie Hartman STRINGS: Bob Barene, Sam Cytron, George Kast, Ray Cerf, °Mischa Russell, Dave Frisina CELESTE: Stan Wrightsman GUITAR: °George Van Eps BASS: Jack Ryan DRUMS: °Nick Fatool VOCAL GROUP: June Hutton, Clark Yocum, Chuck Lowry, Hal Hopper

CONCERTO TO END ALL CONCERTOS
Parts I and II
Composer and arranger: Stan Kenton. Recorded for Capitol July 26, 1946
TRUMPETS: Ray Wetzel, John Anderson, Ken Hanna, Chico Alvarez, Buddy Childers TROMBONES: Kai Winding, Harry Forbes, Miff Sines, Bart Varsalona SAXOPHONES: Al Anthony, Bob Gioga, Boots Mussulli, Vido Musso, Bob Cooper PIANO: Stan Kenton GUITAR: Bob Ahern BASS: Eddie Safranski DRUMS: Shelly Manne

---

I'VE GOT MY LOVE TO KEEP ME WARM
Composer: Irving Berlin. Arranger: Skippy Martin. Recorded for Columbia September 16, 1946
TRUMPETS: Jimmy Zito, Don Paladino, Al Muller, Bob Higgins, Ray Linn TROMBONES: Don Boyd, Ray Klein, Dick Gould, Stumpy Brown SAXOPHONES: Steve Madrick, Mark Douglas, Ted Nash, Eddie Scherr, Butch Stone PIANO: Jeff Clarkson GUITAR: Tony Rizzi BASS: Bob Leininger DRUMS: Dick Shanahan

I SHOULD CARE
Composers: Axel Stordahl and Paul Weston. Lyricist: Sammy Cahn. Arranger: Bill Fine-

---

gan. Recorded for Victor November 14, 1944
TRUMPETS: George Seaberg, Vito Mangano, Dale Pierce, Roger Ellick TROMBONES: Tommy Dorsey, Nelson Riddle, °Benny Benson, Tex Satterwhite TUBA: Joseph Park SAXOPHONES: Sid Cooper, Buddy De Franco, Bruce Branson, Gail Curtis, Al Klink NINE STRINGS: Unknown PIANO: Milt Golden GUITAR: Robert Bain BASS: Sid Block DRUMS: Buddy Rich VOCALS: Bonny Lou Williams, The Sentimentalists (°Peggy, °Ann, Jean and Mary Clark)

HAMP'S WALKIN' BOOGIE
Composer and arranger: Lionel Hampton. Recorded for Decca September 17, 1946
TRUMPETS: Joe Morris, Joe Wilder, Leo Shepard, Wendell Culley, Jimmy Nottingham, Duke Garrette TROMBONES: Jimmy Wormick, Booty Wood, Andrew Penn, Al Hayes SAXOPHONES: Bobby Plater, Ben Kynard, Arnett Cobb, John Griffin, Charlie Fowlkes PIANO: Unknown GUITAR: Billy Mackel BASS: °Charlie Harris, Ted Sinclair DRUMS: Fats Heard VIBRAPHONE: Lionel Hampton

AFTERNOON IN AUGUST
Composer and arranger Bill Stegmeyer. Recorded for Capitol November 10, 1947
TRUMPETS: Billy Butterfield, Archie Johnson, Bobby Peck, Jack Stametz TROMBONES: Keith Butterfield, Ray Jenkins SAXOPHONES: Bill Stegmeyer, Earl Pearson, Norman Elvin, Artie Drelinger PIANO: Mickey Crane GUITAR: Hy White BASS: Sam Bruno DRUMS: Cozy Cole

SHERWOOD'S FOREST
Composer and arranger: Bobby Sherwood. Recorded for Capitol June 18, 1946
TRUMPETS: °Manny Klein, Jack Walker, Don Dean, John Gabel, Ray Downs TROMBONES: Wes Cope, Skip Layton, Bob Leaman, Jim Marshall BASSOON: Merle Bredwell SAXOPHONES: Marty Glaser, Dave Cavanaugh, Seymour Press, Herbie Haymer, Henry Facometta PIANO: Ike Carpenter GUITAR: Bass Hutchinson BASS: Bart Edwards DRUMS: Keith Williams

---

AT SUNDOWN
Composer: Walter Donaldson. Arranger: Bill Finegan. Recorded for Victor October 1, 1946
TRUMPETS: Vito Mangano, George Seaberg, Jack Dougherty, Ziggy Elman, Charlie Shavers TROMBONES: Tommy Dorsey, Charles Larue, Bud Youngman, Ed Benson SAXOPHONES: Louis Prisby, °Abe Most, Boomie Richman, Babe Fresk, Marty Berman PIANO: John Potoker GUITAR: Sam Herman BASS: Sid Block DRUMS: Alvin Stoller

RACHEL'S DREAM
Composer: Benny Goodman. "Head" arrangement. Recorded for Columbia May 7, 1945

CLARINET: Benny Goodman PIANO: Teddy Wilson GUITAR: Mike Bryan BASS: Slam Stewart DRUMS: Morey Feld VIBRAPHONE: Red Norvo

THE MAN WITH THE HORN
Composers: Jack Jenney and Bonnie Lake. Arranger: Unknown. Recorded for Decca July 14, 1947
Same as TENDERLY

BIJOU
Composer and arranger: Ralph Burns. Recorded for Columbia August 8, 1945
TRUMPETS: Conte Candoli, °Pete Candoli, Ray Linn, Sonny Berman, Neal Hefti TROMBONES: Bill Harris, Ralph Pfiffner, Ed Kiefer CLARINET: Woody Herman SAXOPHONES: Sam Marowitz, John La Porta, Flip Phillips, Pete Mondello, Skippy De Sair PIANO: Tony Aless GUITAR: Billy Bauer BASS: Chubby Jackson DRUMS: Dave Tough

ARTISTRY IN RHYTHM
Composer and arranger: Stan Kenton. Recorded for Capitol November 19, 1943
TRUMPETS: Karl George, Buddy Childers, John Carroll, Ray Borden, Dick Morse TROMBONES: Harry Forbes, Bart Varsalona, George Faye SAXOPHONES: Eddie Meyers, Art Pepper, Red Dorris, Maurice Beeson, Bob Gioga PIANO: Stan Kenton GUITAR: Bob Ahern BASS: Clyde Singleton DRUMS: Joe Vernon

LOVER
Composer: Richard Rodgers. Arranger: Eddie Finckel. Recorded for Columbia October 23, 1945
TRUMPETS: Tony Savitt, Tony Russo, Don Fagerquist, Vincent Hughes TROMBONES: Leon Cox, Nick Gaglio, Dick Taylor SAXOPHONES: Harry Terrill, Joe Koch, Buddy Wise, Charlie Ventura, Charlie Kennedy PIANO: Teddy Napoleon GUITAR: Frank Worrell BASS: Irv Lang DRUMS: Gene Krupa

THEN I'LL BE HAPPY
Composer: Cliff Friend. Arranger: Sy Oliver. Recorded for Victor April 8, 1946
TRUMPETS: Vito Mangano, George Seaberg, Jack Dougherty, Ziggy Elman, Charlie Shavers TROMBONES: Tommy Dorsey, Greg Phillips, William Siegel, Tex Satterwhite SAXOPHONES: Sid Cooper, Buddy De Franco, Bruce Branson, Babe Fresk, °Don Lodice PIANO: John Potoker GUITAR: Sam Herman BASS: Sid Block DRUMS: Alvin Stoller

BLOWIN' UP A STORM
Composer: Woody Herman. "Head" arrangement. Recorded for Columbia November 16, 1945
TRUMPETS: Irving Lewis, °Pete Candoli, Shorty Rogers, Sonny Berman, Neal Hefti TROMBONES: Bill Harris, Ralph Pfiffner, Ed Kiefer CLARINET: Woody Herman SAXOPHONES: Sam Marowitz, John La Porta, Flip Phillips, Mickey Folus, Skippy De Sair PIANO: Tony Aless GUITAR: Billy Bauer BASS: Chubby Jackson DRUMS: Don Lamond

HAPPY-GO-LUCKY-LOCAL Parts I and II
Composer and arranger: Duke Ellington. Recorded for Musicraft November 25, 1946
TRUMPETS: Shelton Hemphill, Frank Williams, Taft Jordan, Harold Baker, Cat Anderson, Ray Nance TROMBONES: Claude Jones, Lawrence Brown, Wilbur De Paris SAXOPHONES: Russell Procope, Johnny Hodges, Jimmy Hamilton, Al Sears, Harry Carney PIANO: Duke Ellington GUITAR: Fred Guy BASS: Oscar Pettiford DRUMS: Sonny Greer

THE GOOD EARTH
Composer and arranger: Neal Hefti. Recorded for Columbia August 8, 1945
Same as BIJOU

AUTUMN SERENADE
Composer: Peter De Rose. Arranger: Billy May. Recorded for Columbia July 24, 1945

TRUMPETS: Harry James, Irwin Berken, Jimmy Campbell, Al Ramsey, James Troutman TROMBONES: Vic Hamann, Jess Heath, Charlie Preble, Juan Tizol SAXOPHONES: Willie Smith, Murray Williams, Clint Davis, Corky Corcoran, Stewart Bruner ENGLISH HORN: Corky Corcoran VIOLINS: Robert Bein, Sam Caplan, °John de Voogdt, Sol Gliskin, °Jack Gootkin, George Grossman, Henry Jaworski, Ernest Karpati, Gerson Oberstein, Jerome Reisler VIOLAS: David Uchitel, William Spear, Harold Sorin, Alexander Neiman CELLOS: Carl Zeigler, Elias Friede PIANO: Arnold Ross GUITAR: Hayden Causey BASS: Ed Mihelich DRUMS: Ray Toland

ROUTE 66
Composer and lyricist: Bobby Troup. "Head" arrangement. Recorded for Capitol March 15, 1946
PIANO and VOCAL: °Nat King Cole GUITAR: Oscar Moore BASS: Johnny Miller

CARNEGIE BLUES
Composer and arranger: Duke Ellington. Recorded for Victor January 4, 1945
TRUMPETS: Shelton Hemphill, Taft Jordan, Ray Nance, Cat Anderson TROMBONES: Joe Nanton, Claude Jones, Lawrence Brown CORNET: Rex Stewart SAXOPHONES: Jimmy Hamilton, Otto Hardwick, Johnny Hodges, Al Sears, Harry Carney PIANO: Duke Ellington GUITAR: Fred Guy BASS: Junior Raglin DRUMS: Sonny Greer

LOVER'S LEAP
Composer and arranger: Bob Higgins. Recorded for Columbia February 25, 1946
TRUMPETS: Jimmy Zito, Don Jacoby, Al Muller, Bob Higgins TROMBONES: Bill Forman, Warren Covington, Dick Gould, Stumpy Brown SAXOPHONES: Steve Madrick, Mark Douglas, Ted Nash, Eddie Scherr, Butch Stone PIANO: Jeff Clarkson GUITAR: Bobby Gibbons BASS: Bob Leininger DRUMS: Dick Shanahan

ACKNOWLEDGMENTS

A number of musicians, bandleaders, arrangers, singers, managers, songwriters and others knowledgeable on swing music and other subjects helped with source material for this book. The editors of TIME-LIFE RECORDS wish to thank particularly the following for their assistance: George Barden Jr., John Benson Brooks, Claude Brown, Les Brown, Raymond W. Brown, Warren Brown, Milt Buckner, Ralph Burns, Billy Butterfield, Arnett Cobb, Charles Colin, Stanley Dance, William E. ("Wild Bill") Davison, Maria Cole Devore, Frank Driggs, Eddie Finckel, Bill Finegan, Marvin Fisher, Paul Frehm, Cliff Friend, John Hammond, Lionel Hampton, Gladys Hampton, Bill Harris, Jack Haskell, June Heffernon, Neal Hefti, John Huston, Illinois Jacquet, Quincy Jones, Gene Krupa, Paul Lajoie, Bonnie Lake, Lotte Lenya, Joshua Logan, Johnny Mercer, Eddie Miller, Sam Marowitz, Joe Newman, Red Norvo, Larry Parker, Charles Roman, Marshal Royal, Al Sears, Charlie Shavers, Bobby Sherwood, Eddy Shomer, Jess Stacy, Slam Stewart, Lately Thomas, Bill Titone, Paul Weston, Joe Wilder, Joseph Willicombe Jr., Ralph Young. For picture assistance, Mira Schachne.

Valuable assistance was given by the following departments and individuals of Time Inc.: Anne Drayton and Carmela Lotrecchiano; Library, Benjamin Lightman; Picture Collection, Doris O'Neil; Photographic Laboratory, George Karas and Herbert Orth; TIME-LIFE News Service, Marcia Gauger and Barbara Wilkins.